How to Pass
Professional
Level
Psychometric
Tests

More titles in the Testing series:

www.koganpage.com

You are reading one of the thousands of books published by **Kogan Page**. As Europe's leading independent business book publishers **Kogan Page** has always sought to provide up-to-the-minute books that offer practical guidance at affordable prices.

KoganPage

How to Pass

Professional Level Psychometric Tests

Challenging practice questions for
graduate and professional recruitment

Sam Al-Jajjoka
Third edition

KoganPage

LONDON PHILADELPHIA NEW DELHI

Publisher's note

Every possible effort has been made to ensure that the information contained in this book is accurate at the time of going to press, and the publishers and authors cannot accept responsibility for any errors or omissions, however caused. No responsibility for loss or damage occasioned to any person acting, or refraining from action, as a result of the material in this publication can be accepted by the editor, the publisher or any of the authors.

First published in Great Britain and the United States in 2001 by Kogan Page Limited
Second edition 2004
Third edition 2010
Reissued 2013

120 Pentonville Road	1518 Walnut Street, Suite 1100	4737/23 Ansari Road
London N1 9JN	Philadelphia PA 19102	Daryaganj
United Kingdom	USA	New Delhi 110002
www.koganpage.com		India

© Sam Al-Jajjoka 2001, 2004, 2010, 2013

ISBN   978 0 7494 6795 1
E-ISBN 978 0 7494 6796 8

British Library Cataloguing-in-Publication Data

A CIP record for this book is available from the British Library.

Library of Congress Cataloging-in-Publication Data

Al-Jajjoka, Sam.
    How to pass professional level psychometric tests : challenging practice questions for graduate and professional recruitment / Sam Al-Jajjoka. – 3rd Edition.
        pages cm
    "Reissued 2013."
        ISBN 978-0-7494-6795-1 – ISBN 978-0-7494-6796-8 (ebk.)   1. Information technology–Problems, exercises, etc.   2. Finance–Problems, exercises, etc.
    3. Psychometrics.   I. Title.
        HD30.2.A378 2013
        650.028'7–dc23

                                                                        2012051529

Typeset by Graphicraft Limited, Hong Kong
Printed and bound in India by Replika Press Pvt Ltd

I want to dedicate this third edition to my wife, Taghreed, who is both a surgeon and a mother. She is my closest adviser, friend, and companion, as well as the source of constant encouragement and inspiration.

Contents

Preface

My goal remains to address the needs of those who want to apply for jobs and want to identify their strengths and weaknesses and whether they have specific skills in relation to the job specification or position they are applying for. As well as an increase in content, the third edition incorporates more psychometric tests and more examples to help candidates to practise and familiarize themselves with such tests before their interview or assessment day. I'd like to start by giving you some of my own personal tips on passing and preparing for your assessment day. Before you attend an assessment day, either visit your favourite library or career service, or browse the internet and do some research on the employer and industry that you are considering. Always keep in mind that employers want to see what you can do for them – this is why the employer is inviting you for interview in the first place. The current job market may be the most competitive in recent history: there are simply too many applicants for too few well-paying, skilled positions and it is difficult for the employer to choose amongst thousands of candidates.

Make sure to proofread all your writing carefully before mailing. Have your CV and covering letter read by others. If you find yourself rushing to get something in the mail, take a moment to slow down and make sure you are sending out high-quality information: remember that the employer has to sift through thousands of applications, which is a very difficult job. A scruffy application creates a bad impression. Your career is in your hands.

The employer needs to feel that you took the time and effort to target their company specifically, that you take a special interest in working for them and that you have the abilities and personal qualities to do the job. This is why employers nowadays place such a strong emphasis on psychometric tests as measures of an applicant's skills. Psychometric tests identify your strengths and weaknesses to place you in the appropriate position. They measure whether you have specific abilities or appropriate personal qualities in relation to the job specification and whether you need further training to develop the necessary attributes. Such testing is usually much more effective than interviews alone, according to most psychologists. The accepted view is that putting all the candidates through the same test is a fair way to make a final judgement, but lots of intelligent people may be excluded if their success is to depend on a 20–30 minute test. However, we are living in the real world and Human Resources departments want to produce statistics, so when you call for feedback on your interview they can tell you how you scored compared with other candidates. In this way you are satisfied as you have proof of whether or not you performed to meet the organization's requirements. The employer is also happy because they can argue from a fair position in awarding the job.

If you are unfamiliar with psychometric tests you may be too nervous to do justice to your ability, or may waste valuable time trying to understand what you are being asked to do. You will certainly be at a disadvantage compared with candidates who have already had practice with such tests. This is where this book comes in. It provides you with intelligent tips of the trade and hints that could help to get you a job offer.

I hope this book enhances your understanding of a variety of psychometric tests and that familiarizing yourself with the different tests will give you the courage and self-confidence to perform better. I guarantee that those who read this book will thank me if it helps them to do their best.

Acknowledgements

I owe great debt of gratitude to my readers, mostly graduates from various universities for their immeasurable contribution and invaluable inputs to enhance the quality of this third edition, as well as my software engineer colleagues in Germany, my colleagues and readers in the UK and various professionals for their perceptive comments and judgement.

Introduction

It can be very difficult to separate the careers that suit your personality and abilities from the careers that would irritate you or cause you stress. To be content and successful in a job, you need to ensure that your abilities, competencies and personality are well aligned with those needed for your chosen job and with those of the organization you want to work for. Organizations use many methods to choose the most appropriate candidates for each job, including application forms, references, observation, interviews, group discussion, examples of practical work, written work and psychometric tests.

Psychometric tests are IQ (Intelligence Quotient) tests designed to measure your aptitude for thinking and reasoning. Their use is based on the principle that the best way of predicting job success is to give an individual tasks to do that are representative of the types of thing they might have to do in a particular job, or actual samples of the activities that are carried out in that job. The questions in your psychometric tests, in principle, need no further study or prior knowledge and are based on your logical and analytical abilities. Of course, the more skills that are being tested, the more psychometric tests you will be required to perform and the more accurate and comprehensive will be the picture of you built up by the employer. The aim is to identify your strengths and weaknesses and whether you have specific skills in relation to the job specification or position for which you are being considered. Such testing is usually more effective than interview alone, according to most psychologists. This is why employers nowadays place such a strong emphasis on psychometric tests as a measure of an applicant's abilities. However, it is important to be clear about the nature of psychometric tests that are to be used; for example if you are an existing manager and are applying for a job it is expected that you have developed an aptitude like management skill to some degree and will be able to demonstrate this. If, however, a number of graduates are being assessed for the same position, then it would be unfair to expect them to have the same level of management skill. In this case, the focus would be on their potential to develop management skill with appropriate training.

The most commonly used psychometric tests are verbal and numerical, since they are core elements of most jobs. Other categories include:

- diagrammatic, which involves logical reasoning based on abstract symbols;

- spatial, which requires the visualization of two- and three-dimensional shapes in space;

- programming tests designed to test your logical ability to read and understand material on a new programming language;

- mechanical, where relevant problems are shown in pictorial form; and

- personality tests, which reveal your attitudes and the way you do things and interact with other people and the environment, as well as your motivation, interests and values.

Usually, for graduate positions an assessment centre is set up as the most effective tool for assessing and selecting candidates in both individual and group-based environments. Assessment centres typically involve completing a range of exercises including psychometric tests that simulate the activities carried out in the target job. Some research has shown that assessment centres are the most comprehensive and effective method for predicting successful performance in the job that the candidate is applying for. It is believed by some researchers that assessment centre testing is fairer, objective and consistent, which means that employers and recruiters who can afford to run them are better able to choose the right candidates for the job. If attending one makes you feel a bit nervous, this it is only natural – most people do. A degree of nervousness is not a bad thing as it helps you to keep you alert and sharp throughout the day.

How are psychometric tests constructed?

Typical aptitude psychometric tests are conducted under examination conditions and comprise multi-choice questions, where you shade in or tick the box against the correct answer; they are strictly timed. Each question has only one correct answer, which is often to be selected from three to five alternatives (although there are tests that require more than one suggested answer to be identified as correct). Therefore, every incorrect alternative successfully identified and eliminated improves your chances of choosing the correct answer from the alternatives remaining. The questions become more difficult as you go through and are designed not to be completed within the given time unless you are a genius! You should not be concerned if you do not complete all of a test – it is the number of correct answers that matters.

The test will be standardized in terms of the way it is administered and scored, and may be undertaken using a computer, via the internet or using traditional pen and paper. Your score relates your performance to a 'normed' group. This allows your employer to know how well you can do something in relation to other candidates, the general population, or staff already doing the job, since your score has been gained under exactly the same conditions and the same set of rules. There may also be a 'Pass' mark, whereby if you achieve it you will get the job or the necessary training to do the job, or the employer may have planned to interview a certain number of candidates and your score may put you in this group to go forward to the next stage of selection. On the other hand, your score could simply be a further measure considered by the employer alongside a variety of other measures such as interviews, writing skills, group exercises, leadership ad hoc experience, etc, all of which will be taken into account before making the final decision and might compensate for any weakness in your performance in the psychometric tests. The stage at which tests are taken might give you a clue as to the importance of the results to the employer. The earlier in the selection process you are asked to sit a test, the more important the results are likely to be to the outcome. Employers who use tests only at second interview stage will use them as one of a number of factors. If you have done well on other parts of the selection process then they may make allowances for poor test performance.

So your employer can interpret your score in different ways: individually as a specific ability or aptitude measure, or together with other competencies as part of a general ability measure. This is a very fair way of awarding a job offer, especially in over-applied jobs, as it gives the maximum number of qualified candidates an equal chance to apply for the position without resorting to a lottery.

How to prepare

Well before the test, contact the employer and obtain as much information as possible. What kind of tests will you sit? How long will they take? How are the tests weighted and is negative marking used? Can you use a calculator in numeracy tests? If possible, get them to send you sample tests so you can prepare yourself mentally beforehand. Some organizations send a simple flyer with some practice examples. This is only to give a flavour of what you should expect; it does not mean that only similar tests will be used. While it is sensible to concentrate on those tests, I have known of instances where an organization gave advance warning of only two tests, but surprised candidates on the day with another one, not mentioned in its correspondence.

On the day of a testing session it is important to arrive at the specified location in the best possible physical/mental state. Also, if there is any factor likely to affect your performance, such as disability, you must tell the test administrators before the test. During the test make sure that the physical conditions of the tests room are adjusted so you are comfortable and able to give it your best shot. At the beginning of each test, you are given a couple of examples to ensure you know what you are required to do. Don't hesitate to ask the assessor to clarify the instructions and remove any ambiguity before you start the actual test. Furthermore, on the actual test, if you make a mistake on a test item, you usually will have the chance to work through the question again. However, if you don't understand the instructions, ask immediately for clarification.

Practice makes perfect

Inadvertently you have already carried out most of the preparation! Your education, work experience, personal attainment, general knowledge, know-how skills, etc will have taught you how to think, be analytical, logical and artistic. However, if you feel one of the skills you have learnt is rusty, relearning/practising that skill may improve your performance. For example, if you are required to take a numerical test, it is helpful to brush up your basic mental arithmetic, ie addition, subtraction, multiplication, division, percentages, ratios and how to read graphs and tables. Even basic crosswords, mathematical teasers and number puzzles may help you become used to the comprehension aspects of some tests. Further evidence suggests that some practice of similar tests may improve your performance substantially on actual tests. It is wise to brush up on your exam technique and become more familiar with the types of test you may face. This is where the third edition of this book comes in very handy as it offers invaluable advice on preparing you for the psychometric tests, and provides you with expert tips on how to analyse and make intelligent guesses.

The book contains 20 different timed tests with over 650 practice questions, with answers supplied. The tests are the type of aggressive psychometric tests that may be encountered in IT, management and finance recruitment procedures, although some tests (Chapters 1, 2, 4 and 5) are relevant to other areas of employment too. The book is designed to work in tandem with other publications from Kogan Page, now used by thousands of people.

The book assumes that you have been invited for interview or to an assessment centre, and are preparing yourself for the big day. However, if you have not been invited for interview or to an assessment centre before, you will still find this book really useful. It is designed to be used as a stand-alone guide to test your abilities and the power of your brain to find out more about your strengths and weaknesses. The book also makes the daring assumption that you are somebody special. There are too many books written for every possible candidate (the good, the bad and the ugly): this book is tailored for strong performers like you.

Familiarizing yourself with different tests and utilizing the intelligent tips provided in the book on how to answer the questions for different test will give you the courage and confidence to improve your performance in the actual test. Practice brings mastery. It is like learning a new language: it is difficult to say a word or express your ideas at the beginning, but by practising you become fluent and able to produce your own speech. The investment of time and effort in studying the book and familiarizing yourself with the types of questions that may be asked and tips for approaching them is an investment in your future. Take the time to read through most, if not all of the exercises in this book. There may be exercises that apply directly to your assessment day.

While the exercises in this book are useful to start to teach you the basic skills, feel free, later, to deviate from them and build your own examples to stretch your capability further. Let your examples evolve. They will in all probability get better and better as your brain starts adjusting to a new challenge. Furthermore, speed is an important factor in psychometric tests, but getting the balance between speed and accuracy is essential. Quickly guessing at answers in order to complete the test could work against you, if negative marking is used. On the other hand, if negative marking is not used, utilizing the intelligent tips to eliminate all the wrong answers and using your judgement to choose the best answer from the remaining ones will improve your test scores significantly. Always concentrate on the task you have been set, remembering the rules you have been given. Most wrong answers occur because of carelessness. However, avoid taking too long over a question – skip on to the next one. If you still have time at the end, go back to those you left out. To reflect the time constraints you will face during actual tests, I have suggested a time for the completion of each test. The answers for each test can be found at the end of the relevant chapter, together with an explanation of the answers.

Whereas aptitude tests measure your maximum abilities, personality tests, which strictly speaking are not tests because there are no right or wrong answers, identify your typical reactions and attitudes to a variety of situations and usually are in the form of a questionnaire. Employers know precisely what they are looking for in terms of an ideal personality profile and it is up to you to meet their expectations. For example, they could be trying to identify how well you can interact with others, or your normal reaction to traumatic situations, or just simply your feelings about the kind of people you would like to work with. It is unwise to try to falsify your answers and hide your real personality, because these questions usually have some mechanism for internal checking, whereby the same questions are asked with slightly different wording early and late in the test to try to detect dishonest answers. Ultimately, there is little point in pretending to be the kind of employee an organization is looking for if that is not the case. If you manage to cheat the system, you could end up being accepted for a job to which your character is unsuited, resulting in a discontented you and an unhappy employer. For more information on personality tests, see the list of titles offered by Kogan Page at the end of this book.

Finally, always, even if you fail, ask the employer for feedback about your performance. This may help you to pinpoint your weaknesses so you can work on them in the future and learn from the experience; it may also aid you in deciding your career path.

General remarks about your psychometric test day

- Discuss your test with your career adviser (if you have one), who might suggest you sit a timed practice test prior to your actual test day. Such practice is nowadays available in most universities to give you some feedback on your performance, so you know what you should work on before the actual test.

- Acquaint and familiarize yourself with what is required, by hard work and practice prior to the test; this will help you to improve your performance.

- Avoid being nervous; believe in yourself.

- At the beginning of each test you are given a couple of examples to ensure you know what you are required to do. Don't hesitate to ask the assessor to clarify the instructions and remove any ambiguity.

- The best way to choose alternatives in multiple-choice tests is to eliminate all the wrong answers and use your judgement to choose the best answer from the remaining ones.

- To meet the test requirements, particular care should be taken with the way you record your answers in the answer sheet. Apply the rules exactly. If you are asked to put a cross in the chosen box, you should do exactly that; anything else might be marked as incorrect even though you might have answered the question correctly.

- Always do your rough work on separate scrap paper and don't mark your question book or the answer sheet unnecessarily.

- Work as quickly and accurately as you can and avoid taking too long over a question; if you have time left at the end, go back and try it again. Remember, you don't get extra marks for finishing early and it is only the number of correct answers that counts. Sometimes negative marking is used, which means that you lose marks for incorrect answers. If this is the case, don't use guesswork to fill in your score sheet, and try your best to answer correctly as many items as possible. However, if negative marking is not used, I advise the use of intelligent guessing to improve your score, by eliminating all the incorrect choices and making guesses on the remaining ones.

Chapter 1
Psychometric tests for IT and finance

Diagrammatic reasoning using the alphabet

In this test you are shown a number of diagrams representing an input → transformation → output process in which the input is altered by rules depending on commands, which are represented by symbols. Your task is to identify the rule represented by each symbol, based on the information in the diagram, and to apply these rules to the input data you are given. Different rules may be used for the same symbol in different diagrams, so consider each diagram on its own and work out what rule each symbol stands for; don't generalize the rules for the whole test. No two different symbols have the same rules in the same diagram. As a rule of thumb always follow the arrow for input and output for every path independently. Table 1.1 shows some of the common rules used in alphabetic diagrammatic reasoning. It is only to give an idea about what to expect; other possibilities are left to your imagination.

TABLE 1.1   Some common alphabetic diagrammatic reasoning rules

	Input	Output	Comment
1	ABCD	ABC	Delete right
2	ABCD	BCD	Delete left
3	ABCD	ABD	Delete third from left
4	ABCD	ACD	Delete second from left
5	ABCD	DABC	Last is first
6	ABCD	BCDA	First is last
7	ABCD	ABDC	Exchange the position of the last two characters
8	ABCD	ACBD	Exchange the position of the middle two characters
9	ABCD	DCBA	Move sequence to the front
10	ABCD	DBCA	Exchange the first and last
11	ABCD	ABCDF	Add a new character F to the sequence
12	ABCD	AABCD	Add similar character to the first
13	ABCD	ABCE	Change the last character to what follows in the alphabetical sequence
14	ABCD	CDAB	Change every two characters from left to right

Tips

Consider the example shown in Figure 1.1 and follow the rules as one way to solve the problem:

- Identify the shortest path by following only one input and output path. In Figure 1.1 we have three paths: path 1 and path 2 are the shortest and path 3 is the longest.

- Identify all the identical symbols; if identical symbols appear in one diagram, they must obey the same rules.

- Work out the shortest path rules, ie path 1 and path 2 using Table 1.1 as your guide, as shown in Figure 1.2. As you can see, once you have figured out the rules for one symbol you can apply the same rules straight away to other occurrences of that symbol in the same diagram. By doing this you will save time.

- In any one diagram, two different symbols do not have the same rules.

- Finally go back to the longest path 3, and as you can see you are left to find out the rules for only one symbol, #. Again, consider the common rules introduced in Table 1.1 in conjunction with the other symbols as shown in Figure 1.2.

Once you have mastered the basics, try to define your own symbols and rules and devise new diagrams to suit your ability and convenience. However, I am sure that as you become more familiar with the diagrams you will be able to create your own way and devise a new method to solve the problem that suits your ability.

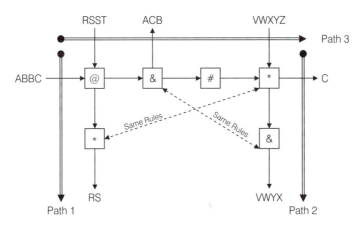

FIGURE 1.1   The three paths

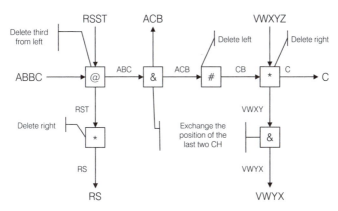

FIGURE 1.2   Step-by-step solution

Now try the following practice questions in Figures 1.3 to 1.9, which contain 40 questions in all. Mark your answers on scrap paper see how many questions you can do in 30 minutes.

Figure 1.3

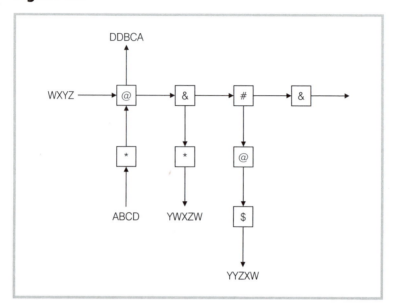

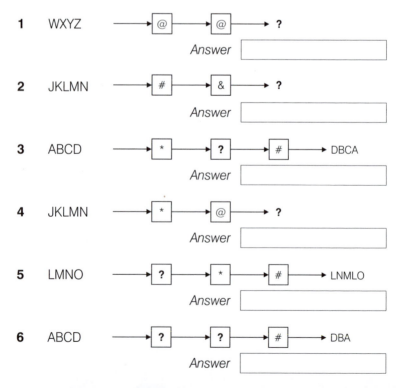

Figure 1.4

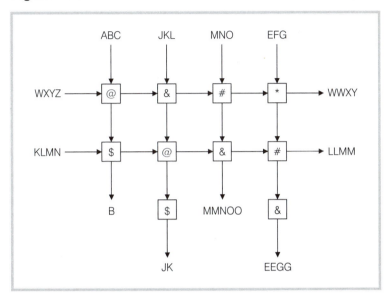

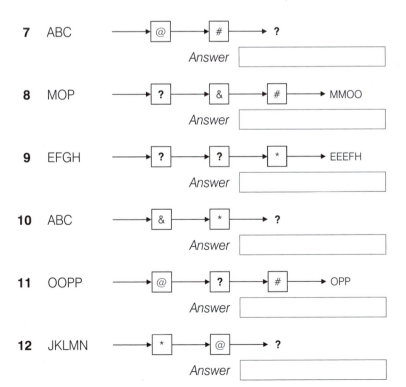

Figure 1.5

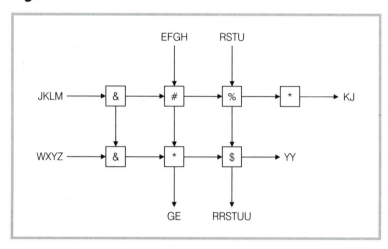

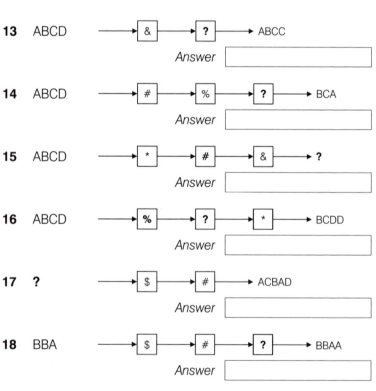

Figure 1.6

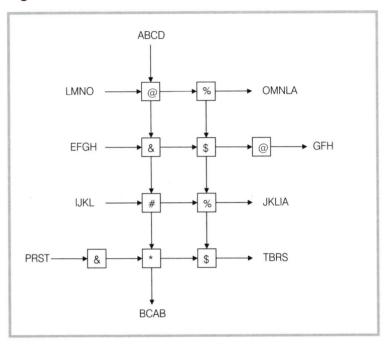

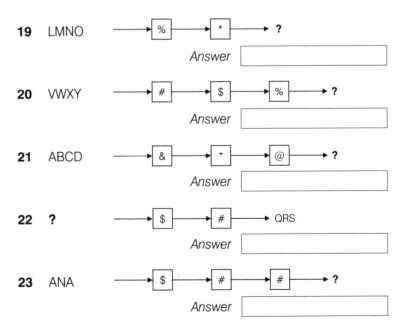

Figure 1.7

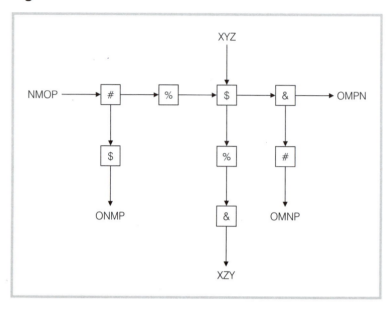

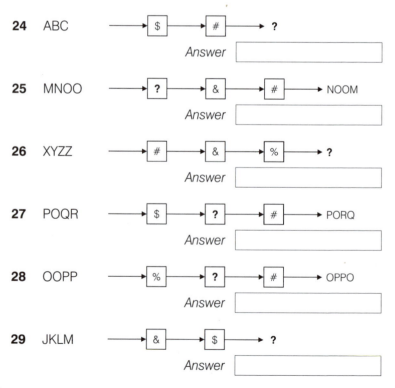

Figure 1.8

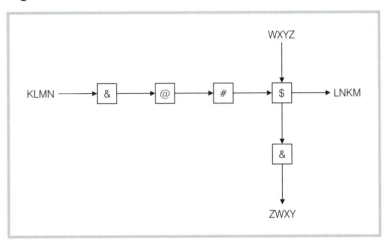

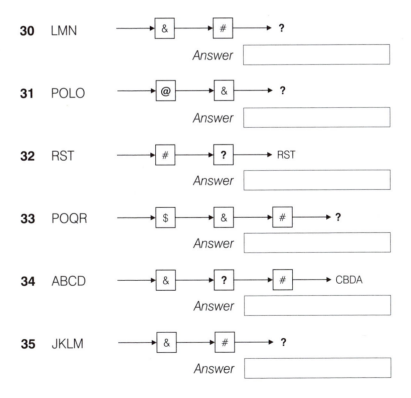

30 LMN   → & → # → ?

Answer

31 POLO   → @ → & → ?

Answer

32 RST   → # → ? → RST

Answer

33 POQR   → $ → & → # → ?

Answer

34 ABCD   → & → ? → # → CBDA

Answer

35 JKLM   → & → # → ?

Answer

Figure 1.9

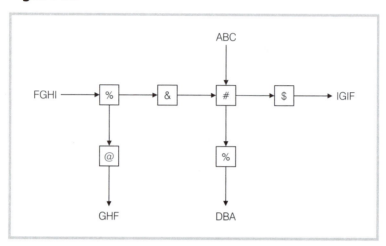

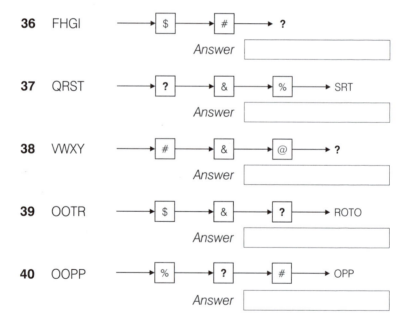

Diagrammatic reasoning using shapes

In this case you are shown a number of diagrams in which a shape (in a square box) is altered by a command represented by a symbol (we use similar symbols as before; however they are put in circles rather than squares). Table 1.2 shows some of the common rules used, just to give you an idea of what you should expect. Be aware that these are not the only possibilities.

TABLE 1.2   Some common rules used in diagrammatic reasoning using shapes

	Shape	Altered	Comment
1			Change of size
2			Change of colour
3			Change of shape
4			Rotate to any angle
5			Add horizontal line
6			Add vertical line
7			Turn only the colour upside down

Tips

Consider the example shown in Figure 1.10 and follow these simple rules as one way to solve the problem:

● Identify the shortest path by following only one input → output path. In Figure 1.10 we have only two equal paths, to consider at the same time. Follow the rules represented by each symbol and see the solution in Figure 1.11.

● Identify similar symbols; since they are in one diagram, they must obey the same rules. However, a symbol may well have a different meaning in another figure, so avoid generalization in your test.

● In any one diagram, two different symbols do not have the same rules.

● The same symbol may appear twice in a sequence in a single figure. The symbol may, for example, convert the shape from square to circle, but the second time the same symbol converts it back again, which is different from the rules used in diagrammatic reasoning using the alphabet.

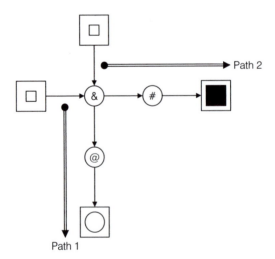

FIGURE 1.10   The two paths

I am sure that as you become more familiar with the diagrams you will be able to create your own way and devise a new method to solve the problem that suits your ability.

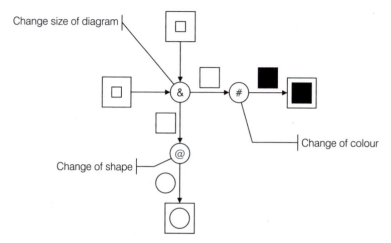

FIGURE 1.11   The solution to the example in Figure 1.10

Now try the practice questions shown in Figures 1.12 to 1.15, which contain 24 questions. Mark your answers on a scrap paper and see how many questions you can do in 15 minutes.

Figure 1.12

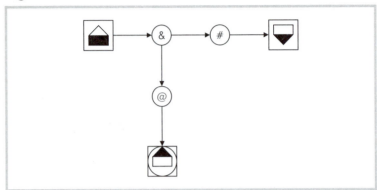

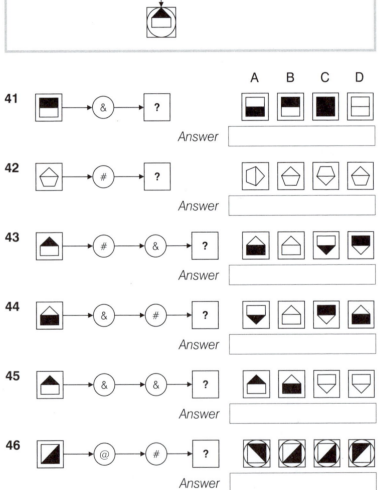

Figure 1.13

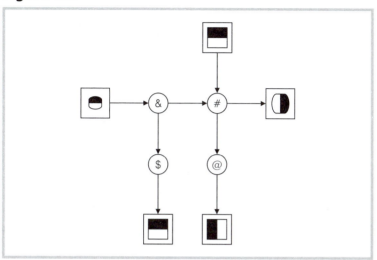

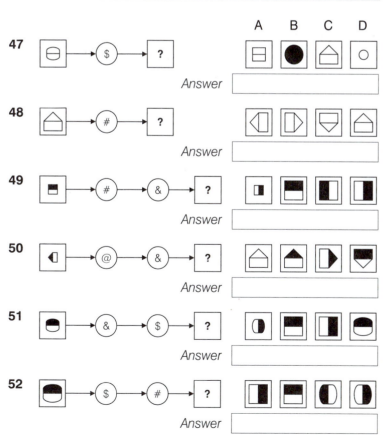

Figure 1.14

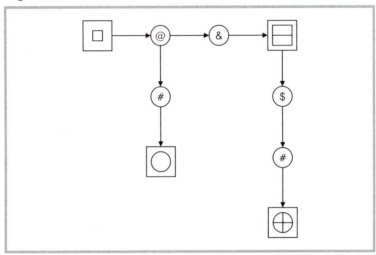

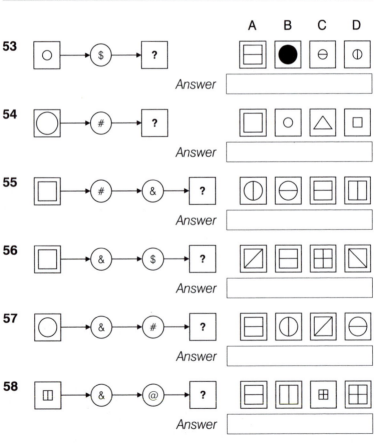

Figure 1.15

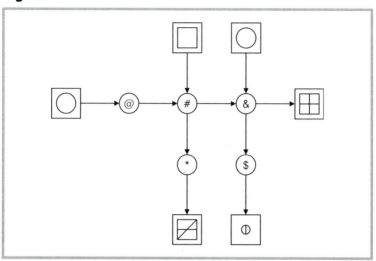

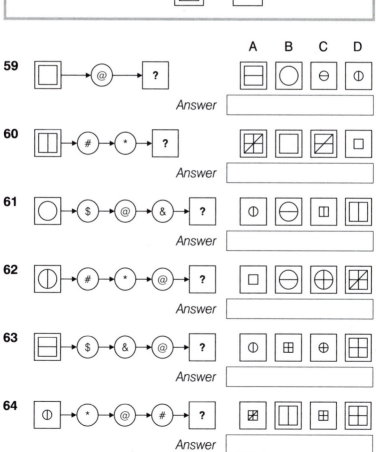

Diagrammatic reasoning using control process boxes

The test consists of four control process or transformation boxes and a control flow arrow inside a rectangle. Each box is responsible for a certain process for changing a shape. These processes, from top to bottom, are defined in Figure 1.16.

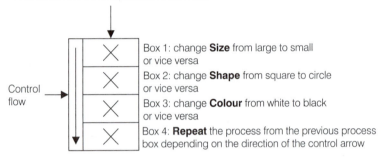

A cross means the box process is activated

Control flow

Box 1: change **Size** from large to small or vice versa

Box 2: change **Shape** from square to circle or vice versa

Box 3: change **Colour** from white to black or vice versa

Box 4: **Repeat** the process from the previous process box depending on the direction of the control arrow

FIGURE 1.16   The order of the four control process boxes and the transformations they apply

The order of the process boxes, from box 1 to box 4, is constant throughout the test. The box is activated (enabled) only when it has a cross inside, otherwise the operation of that particular box is ignored. In other words, all transformation of the data flow to it is ignored. To trigger a process box is to activate it (to put a cross in it) so that it carries out its transformation process. The control flow arrow is responsible for the direction of the transformation process, either from box 1 to box 4 or from box 4 to box 1, as illustrated in the example in Figure 1.17. As you can see, the output of the development of the shape, ie a square in this case, is dissimilar, even though we have activated the same process boxes. This is due to the direction of the control flow arrow.

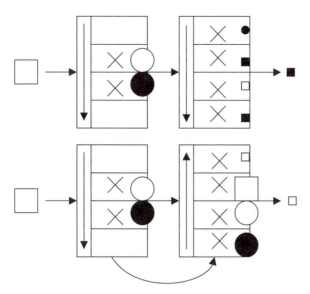

FIGURE 1.17   The effect of the control flow arrow

Tips

- Identify the direction of the control flow arrow. This will help you to decide whether to process the boxes from top to bottom or vice versa.

- Pay special attention to box 4 (the repeat box). If activated (crossed) it can either repeat the process of box 3 (change colour) or box 1 (change size), depending on the direction of the control arrow.

- Bear in mind that an uncrossed box means an inactivated process and should be ignored.

Start the test when you have understood the basic concept of the requirements, using Figure 1.16 as your guide. The diagrammatic reasoning using control process boxes consists of Test 1 and Test 2 with 20 questions for each. In Test 1, you have to decide the least number of process boxes that should be activated (crossed) in order to achieve the output transformation shape. In Test 2, you have to select one output transformation shape from four given choices, ie A, B, C and D. In both tests the last 10 questions are more difficult because the control arrow takes different directions. You have 25 minutes to complete both tests.

Test 1

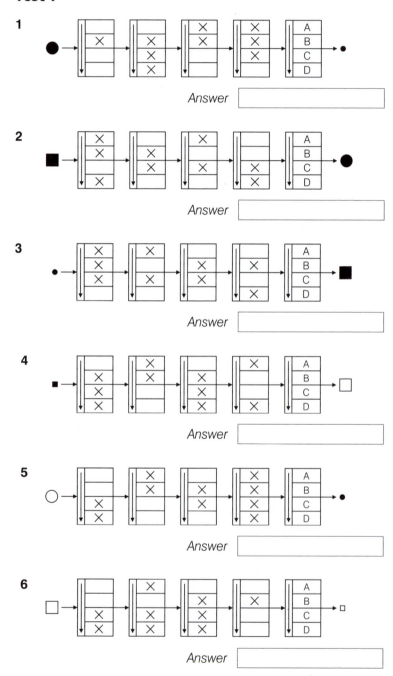

1

Answer

2

Answer

3

Answer

4

Answer

5

Answer

6

Answer

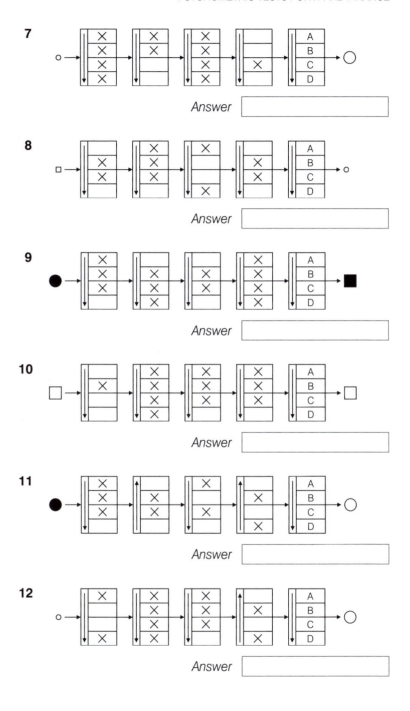

7

Answer

8

Answer

9

Answer

10

Answer

11

Answer

12

Answer

13

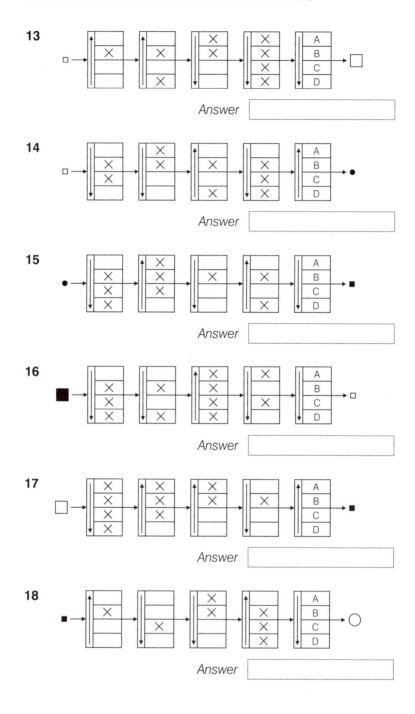

Answer

14

Answer

15

Answer

16

Answer

17

Answer

18

Answer

19

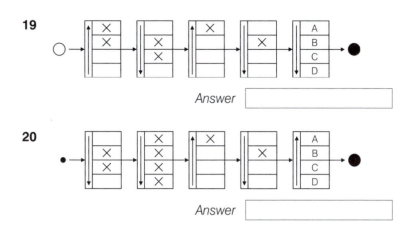

Answer

20

Answer

Test 2

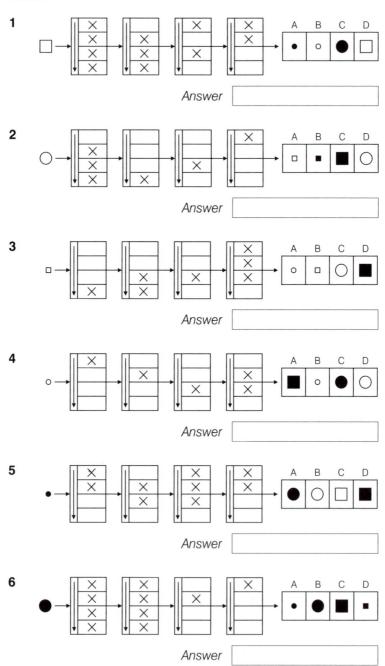

1

Answer

2

Answer

3

Answer

4

Answer

5

Answer

6

Answer

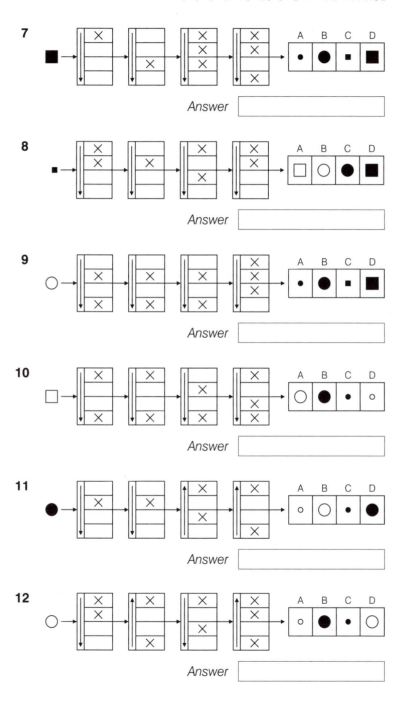

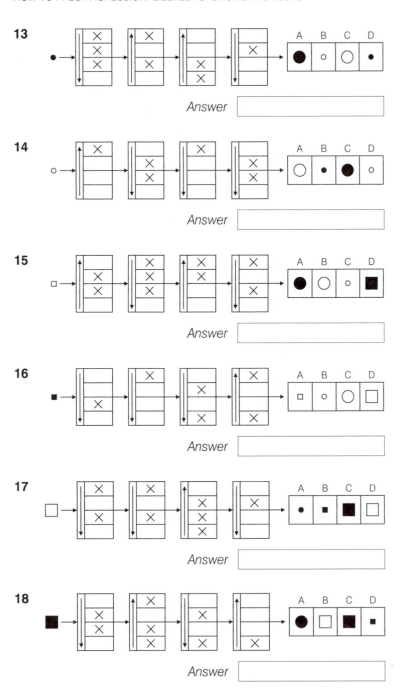

13

Answer

14

Answer

15

Answer

16

Answer

17

Answer

18

Answer

19

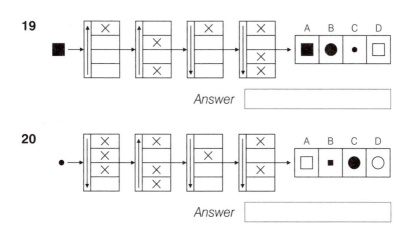

Answer

20

Answer

Diagrammatic reasoning using columns of boxes

In this test the commands are represented by symbols in boxes attached to octagons arranged in columns. A complete list of these commands and what they do is shown in Figure 1.18.

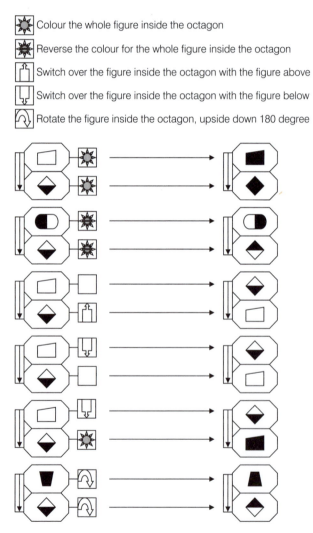

FIGURE 1.18   A complete list of commands, what they do and examples

Tips

● Always start at the top of the column and work down.

● Deal with each command in turn to find which of the four alternative columns is the correct answer in the test.

● Bear in mind that an empty box without a symbol means an inactivated command and should have no effect.

Start the test when you have understood the basic concept of the test requirements as shown in the example in Figure 1.18. The diagrammatic reasoning test using columns of boxes consists of 24 questions and you have to select one output alternative from four given choices, ie A, B, C and D. You have 12 minutes to complete the test.

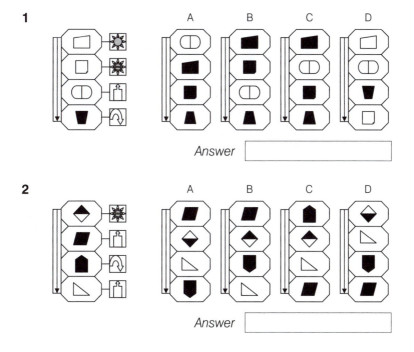

Answer

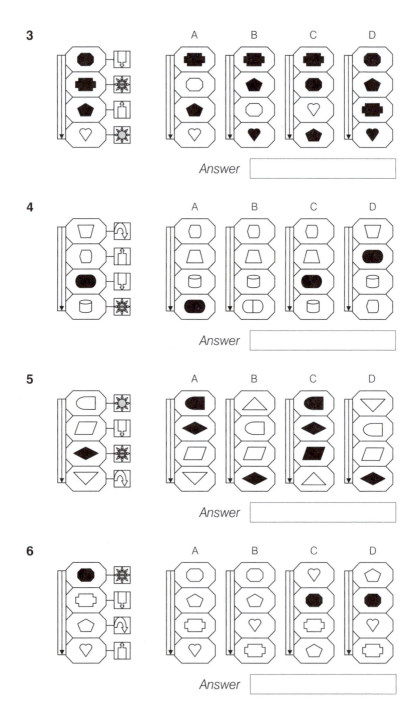

3

A   B   C   D

Answer [   ]

4

A   B   C   D

Answer [   ]

5

A   B   C   D

Answer [   ]

6

A   B   C   D

Answer [   ]

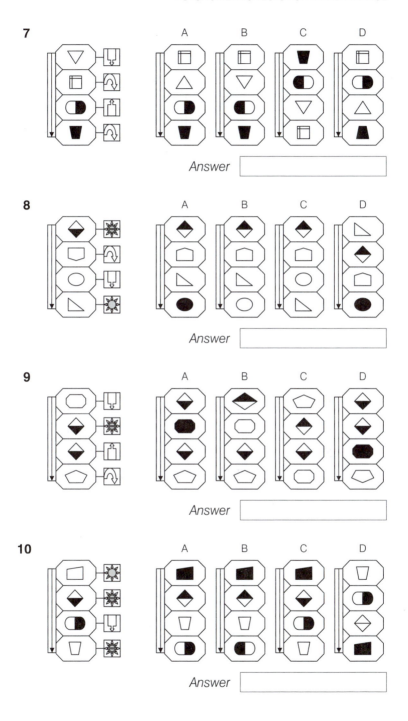

7

A   B   C   D

Answer

8

A   B   C   D

Answer

9

A   B   C   D

Answer

10

A   B   C   D

Answer

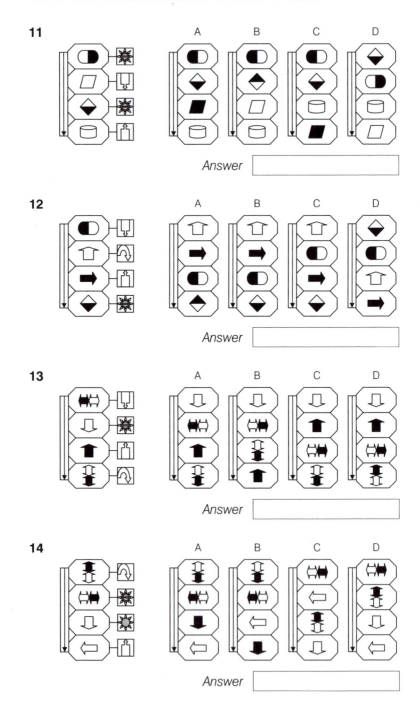

11   A   B   C   D

Answer

12   A   B   C   D

Answer

13   A   B   C   D

Answer

14   A   B   C   D

Answer

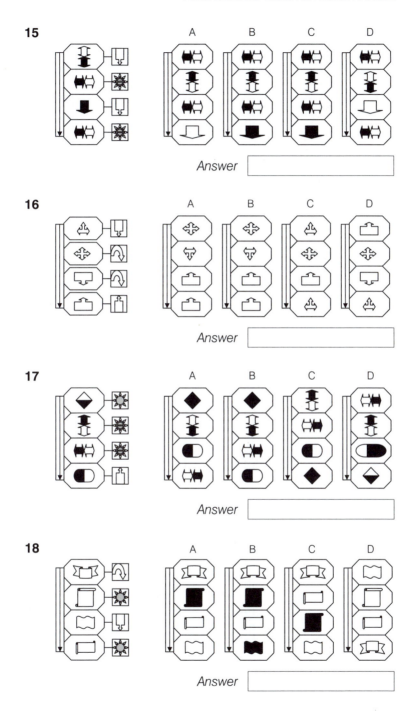

15

A   B   C   D

Answer

16

A   B   C   D

Answer

17

A   B   C   D

Answer

18

A   B   C   D

Answer

19

20

21

22

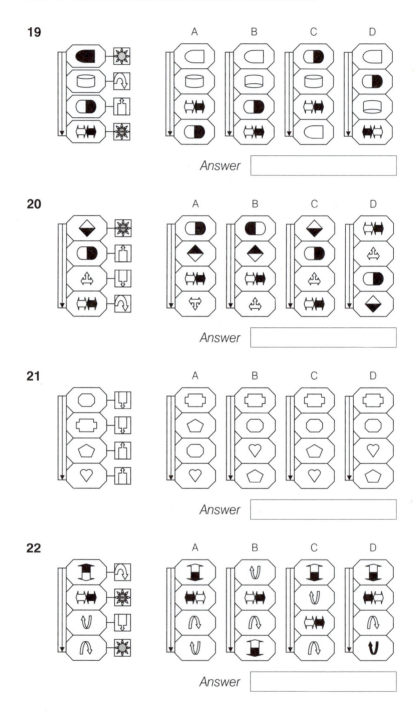

Answer

Answer

Answer

Answer

A   B   C   D

23

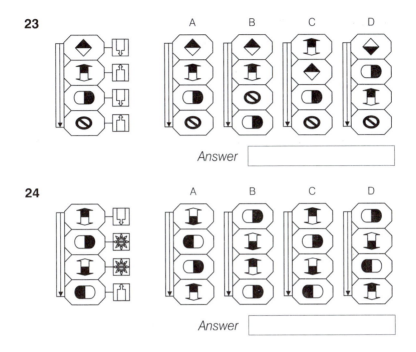

Answer [   ]

24

Answer [   ]

Solutions for Chapter 1

Diagrammatic reasoning using the alphabet

FIGURE 1.3

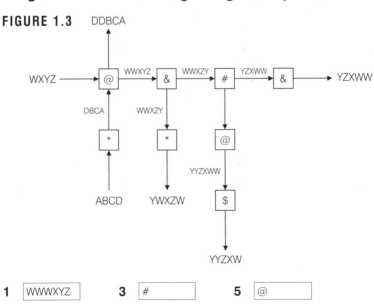

1	WWWXYZ		3	#		5	@
2	NMLJK		4	NNKLMJ		6	&, $

FIGURE 1.4

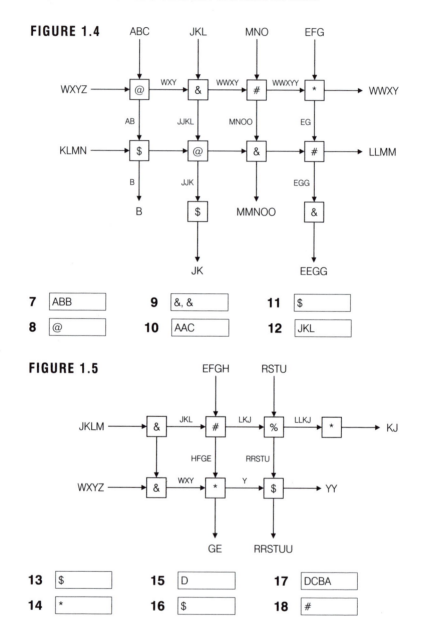

7	ABB	9	&, &	11	$
8	@	10	AAC	12	JKL

FIGURE 1.5

13	$	15	D	17	DCBA
14	*	16	$	18	#

FIGURE 1.6

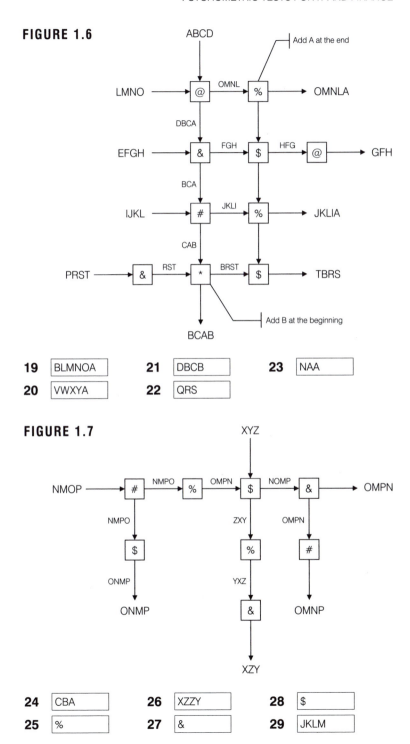

19	BLMNOA	21	DBCB	23	NAA
20	VWXYA	22	QRS		

FIGURE 1.7

24	CBA	26	XZZY	28	$
25	%	27	&	29	JKLM

FIGURE 1.8

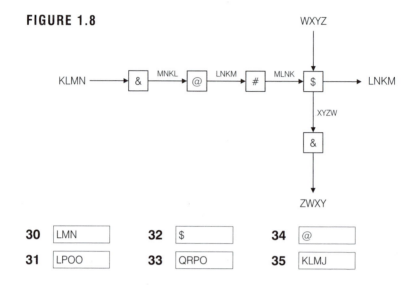

30	LMN	**32**	$	**34**	@
31	LPOO	**33**	QRPO	**35**	KLMJ

FIGURE 1.9

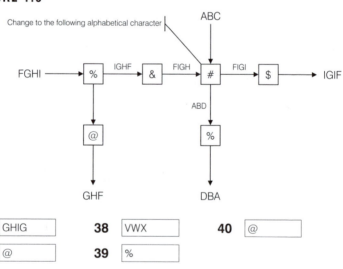

36	GHIG	**38**	VWX	**40**	@
37	@	**39**	%		

PSYCHOMETRIC TESTS FOR IT AND FINANCE

Diagrammatic reasoning using shapes – solutions

FIGURE 1.12

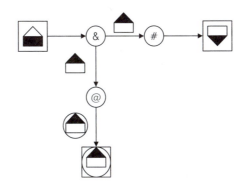

41	A	**43**	D	**45**	A
42	C	**44**	A	**46**	A

FIGURE 1.13

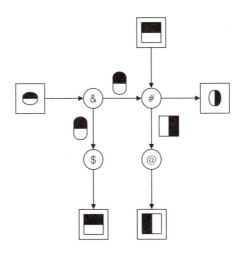

47	A	**49**	D	**51**	B
48	B	**50**	C	**52**	A

FIGURE 1.14

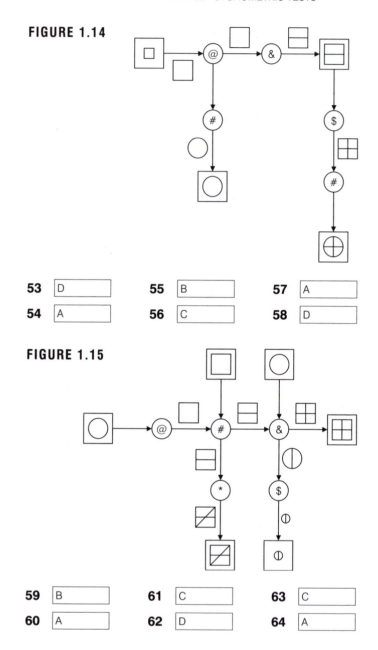

53	D	**55**	B	**57**	A
54	A	**56**	C	**58**	D

FIGURE 1.15

59	B	**61**	C	**63**	C
60	A	**62**	D	**64**	A

Diagrammatic reasoning using control process boxes

Test 1 – solutions

The least number of process boxes that should be activated in order to achieve the output transformation shape are indicated by the crosses in the final column.

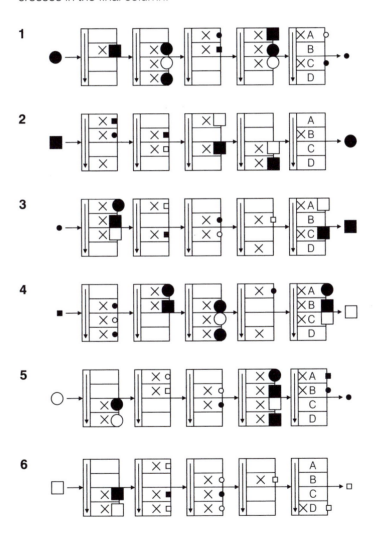

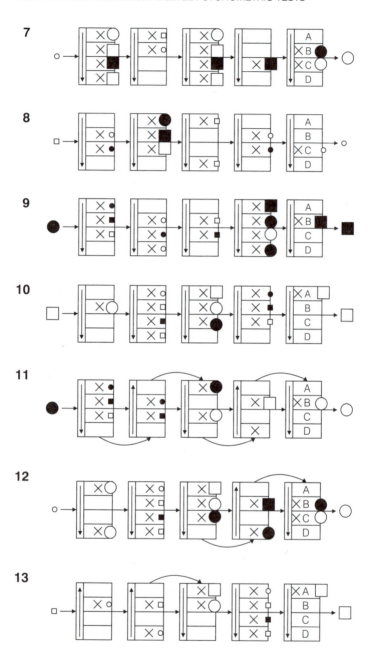

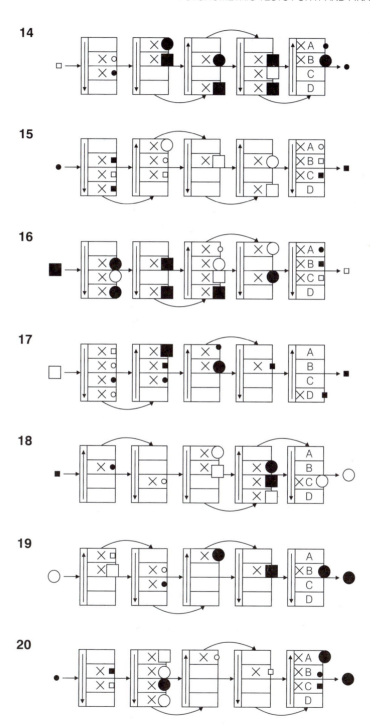

Test 2 – solutions

The letter (A, B, C or D) denoting the correct output transformation shape is encircled in the following solutions.

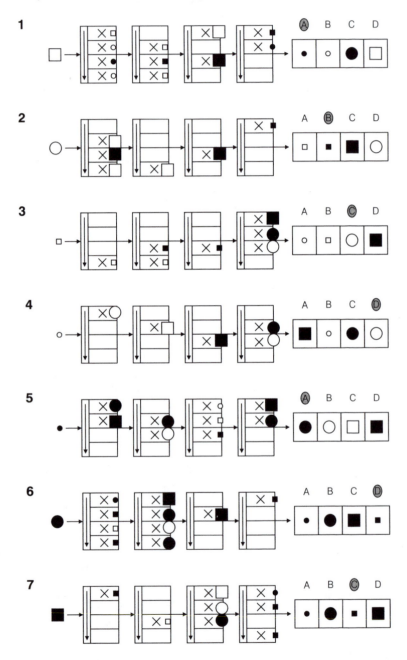

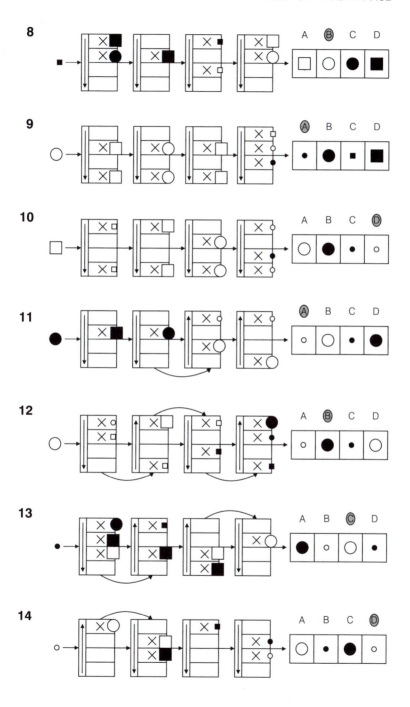

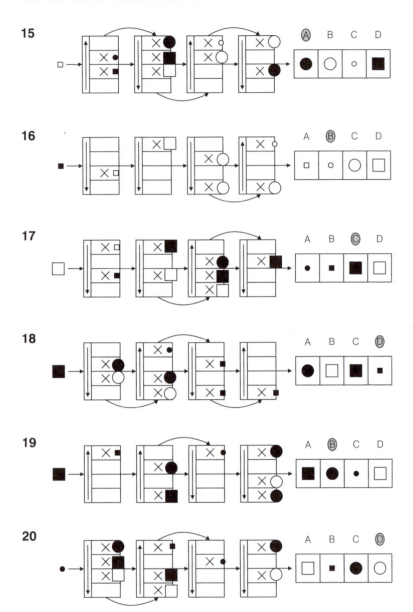

Diagrammatic reasoning using columns of boxes – solutions

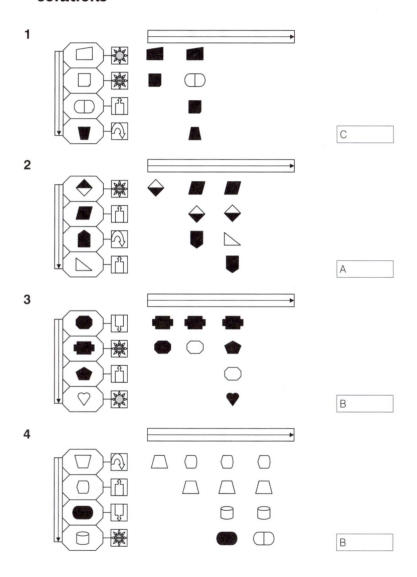

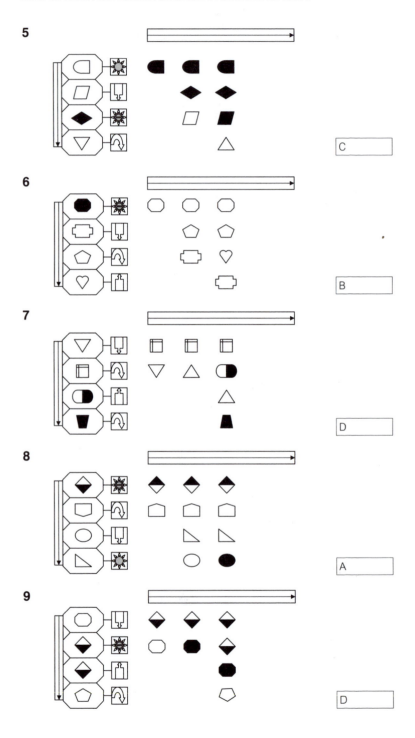

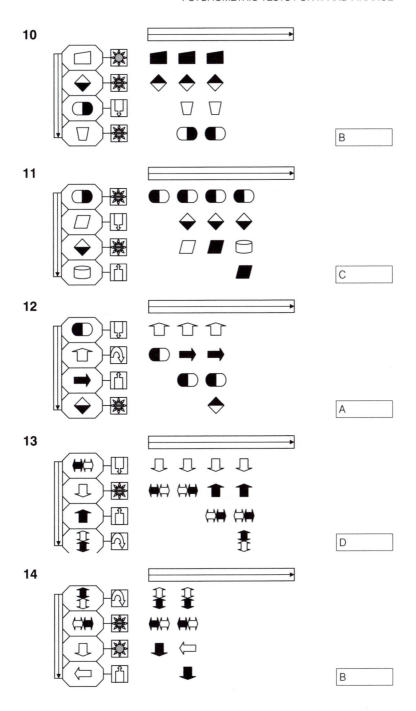

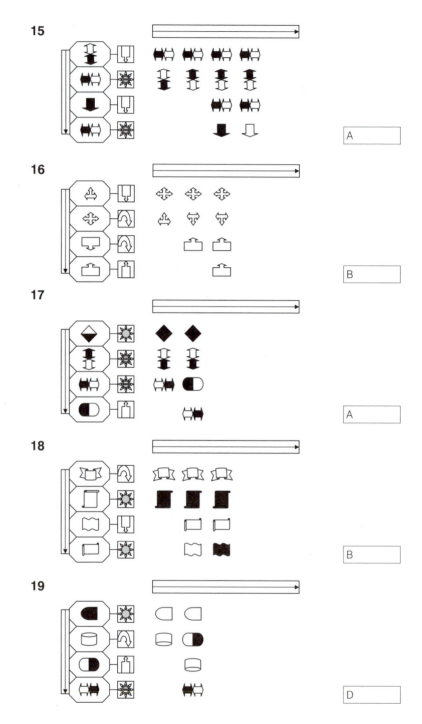

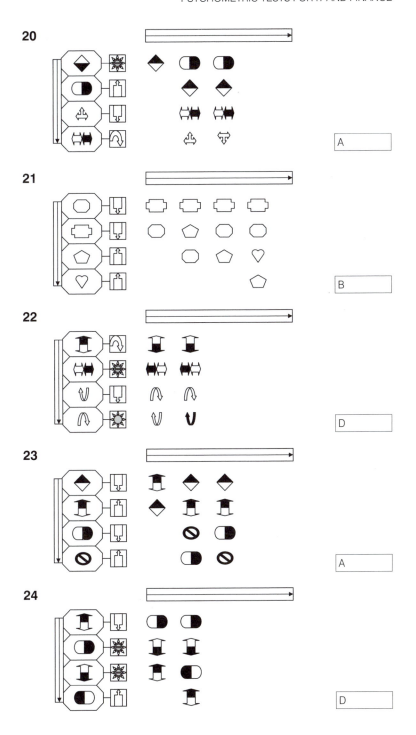

Chapter 2
Psychometric tests for finance and management

Number series

This type of test is popular and used extensively in recruitment to test basic numerical reasoning abilities. The test consists of a sequence of numbers and your task is to find out the pattern and progression of the sequences, then find the number to replace the question mark (?) in the sequences, by selecting one from four provided choices, as illustrated below:

Example 1

9	18	36	?

A	B	C	D
72	59	63	54

In this sequence each number is increased by multiplying by 2:
9 (×2) = 18 (×2) = 36 (×2) = ? = 72, therefore the answer is A.

Example 2

29	2	31	33	?

A	B	C	D
63	64	2	54

In this sequence the two previous numbers are added to obtain the next number in the series: 31 is obtained by adding 29 + 2; 33 is obtained by adding 2 + 31. Therefore ? is equal to 31 + 33 = 64, therefore the answer is B.

Tips

● I have provided in this test most of the common types of series you might expect in your actual test. I suggest you first attempt and take the test within the time limit, then go to the end of the chapter where you will find the answers and learn how the different series of numbers are constructed. After you feel confident that you have understood all the basic principles, take the test again and see the differences by comparing your results with the first attempt.

● This test deals with basic principles of arithmetic and you have to use quick mental arithmetic to answer the questions; usually, calculators are not allowed in this test. I recommend that you read the tips on numerical estimation tests in Chapter 5 to help you to develop the quick mental arithmetic skills necessary to improve your speed and performance.

Now try the number series test below, which consists of 40 questions, without the use of a calculator, and see how many you can answer in 10 minutes by selecting one of the four choices, ie A, B, C or D. Mark your answer on a sheet of paper and compare your results with the answers provided at the end of this chapter.

							A	B	C	D

1 | 2 | 8 | 14 | ? | 26 |

| 19 | 20 | 18 | 21 |

Answer

2 | 3 | 6 | ? | 24 | 48 |

| 12 | 10 | 14 | 16 |

Answer

3 | 19 | 16 | ? | 10 | 7 |

| 11 | 12 | 13 | 14 |

Answer

4 | 81 | 27 | 9 | ? | 1 |

| 4 | 1 | 2 | 3 |

Answer

5 | 0.5 | 1.1 | ? | 2.3 | 2.9 |

| 1.7 | 1.5 | 1.4 | 1.3 |

Answer

6 | 1.9 | 3.8 | 7.6 | ? | 30.4 |

| 15.2 | 13.2 | 16.4 | 14.2 |

Answer

7 | 9 | 10 | 12 | 15 | 19 | ? |

| 26 | 22 | 23 | 24 |

Answer

8 | ? | 22 | 16 | 11 | 7 | 4 |

| 33 | 31 | 29 | 28 |

Answer

9 | 29 | 19 | 48 | 67 | ? |

| 88 | 115 | 114 | 108 |

Answer

10 | 2 | 5 | 10 | ? | 500 |

| 60 | 300 | 50 | 100 |

Answer

		A	B	C	D

11 | 4 | ? | 16 | 32 | 64 |

| 6 | 12 | 10 | 8 |

Answer [ ]

12 | 3 | 3 | ? | 18 | 72 |

| 6 | 18 | 9 | 8 |

Answer [ ]

13 | ? | 36 | 34 | 33 | 33 |

| 37 | 38 | 39 | 41 |

Answer [ ]

14 | 72 | ? | 6 | 3 | 3 |

| 24 | 26 | 54 | 18 |

Answer [ ]

15 | 9 | 4 | 5 | 1 | 2 | ? |

| −1 | 3 | 1 | 4 |

Answer [ ]

16 | 17 | 18 | 16 | 19 | 15 | ? |

| 20 | 17 | 22 | 14 |

Answer [ ]

17 | 37 | 36 | 38 | 35 | 39 | 34 | ? |

| 42 | 38 | 36 | 40 |

Answer [ ]

18 | 8 | 16 | 18 | ? | 38 |

| 30 | 26 | 24 | 36 |

Answer [ ]

19 | 11 | 13 | 39 | ? | 123 |

| 81 | 41 | 61 | 72 |

Answer [ ]

20 | 13 | 10 | 30 | ? | 81 |

| 32 | 45 | 27 | 29 |

Answer [ ]

		A	B	C	D

21 | 2 | 6 | 3 | 9 | 13 | 10 | ? | 34 | | 30 | 14 | 29 | 18 |

Answer [   ]

22 | 8 | 24 | 12 | 14 | 42 | 21 | ? | 69 | | 24 | 23 | 43 | 33 |

Answer [   ]

23 | 3 | 12 | 11 | 44 | 43 | ? | | 45 | 47 | 72 | 172 |

Answer [   ]

24 | 6 | 10 | 13 | 11 | 15 | 18 | 16 | ? | | 23 | 21 | 20 | 17 |

Answer [   ]

25 | 2 | 8 | 4 | 16 | 4 | 16 | 8 | ? | 8 | | 16 | 32 | 4 | 24 |

Answer [   ]

26 | 25 | 5 | 25 | 30 | 6 | 30 | 35 | ? | | 8 | 9 | 7 | 32 |

Answer [   ]

27 | 1 | 2 | 4 | 2 | 4 | 6 | ? | | 6 | 3 | 4 | 1 |

Answer [   ]

28 | 16 | 8 | 32 | 16 | 64 | ? | 128 | | 32 | 80 | 96 | 72 |

Answer [   ]

29 | 7 | 12 | 24 | 29 | ? | 63 | | 24 | 34 | 45 | 58 |

Answer [   ]

30 | 1 | 3 | 3 | 18 | 18 | ? | | 90 | 72 | 36 | 162 |

Answer [   ]

			A	B	C	D

31 | 1 | 1 | 3 | 3 | 7 | 9 | 13 | ? | | 27 | 17 | 19 | 21 |

Answer [ ]

32 | 9 | 1.5 | 6 | 3 | 3 | 6 | 0 | ? | | 1 | 6 | 9 | 12 |

Answer [ ]

33 | 1 | 8 | 27 | 64 | 125 | ? | | 96 | 116 | 216 | 210 |

Answer [ ]

34 | 3 | –9 | 27 | –81 | ? | | 243 | 162 | 180 | 198 |

Answer [ ]

35 | 7 | 9 | 13 | 21 | 37 | ? | | 41 | 47 | 69 | 57 |

Answer [ ]

36 | 67 | 13 | 54 | 87 | 26 | 61 | 23 | 1 | ? | | 22 | 88 | 24 | 42 |

Answer [ ]

37 | 81 | 0.5 | 9 | 0.75 | 1 | 1 | ? | | 0.11 | 1.25 | 0.75 | 2 |

Answer [ ]

38 | 33 | 32 | 34 | 31 | 35 | 30 | 36 | 29 | ? | | 33 | 37 | 39 | 41 |

Answer [ ]

39 | 69 | 96 | 33 | 11 | 11 | 33 | ? | 69 | | 93 | 66 | 96 | 63 |

Answer [ ]

40 | 79 | 8 | 87 | 95 | 182 | ? | | 277 | 212 | 192 | 276 |

Answer [ ]

Character series

Character series is one of the tests commonly used by large organizations instead of number series. My advice is to be prepared for both in case the organization does not tell you which one it will use. In this test you will be presented with a character series and you are asked to find the correct rules and complete the series. A series can start from any point in the alphabet (A–Z) and you have to work out which sequences to use.

Tips

For many candidates, character series tests offer the opportunity to add extra points to their overall performance during the assessment day. Write the alphabetical series (A–Z) on a separate scrap of paper to help you visualize the order of all the characters and then work out the sequences as quickly and accurately as possible. I personally wrote the sequences about five times during the practice session on separate paper, so if I marked one erroneously, I would already have another one available without using a rubber. Look at the examples below.

Example 1

				1	2	3	4	5
X Y X Y X Y X Y				X	Y	Z	V	W

For this example, the series goes: XY, XY, XY. The next letter in the series is X – choice 1.

Example 2

				1	2	3	4	5
V V W W X X Y Y				U	S	T	Z	Q

In example 2, the series goes like this: VV, WW, XX, YY. The next letter in the series is Z – choice 4.

Now try example 3 and indicate the correct answer on a separate piece of paper.

Example 3

```
                              1   2   3   4   5
    V   J   W   J   X   J   Y   J    L   M   Z   O   P
```

In example 3, the series goes: VJ, WJ, XJ, YJ. Therefore, the correct answer is Z – choice 3.

Finally, do example 4 and indicate the correct answer, which is one of the letters to the right of the box.

Example 4

```
                                  1   2   3   4   5
    a   b   c   d   a   b   c   d   a   b   c    d   a   b   c   e
```

In example 4, the series goes like this: abcd, abcd, abc. Therefore, the correct answer is d – choice 1.

When you are ready and confident that you have understood the concept, try the 36 practice questions and allow yourself eight minutes to finish.

1 2 3 4 5

1 | B | B | C | D | D | E | F | F | | C | H | G | K | I |

Answer [   ]

2 | M | S | M | T | N | S | N | T | O | | O | T | S | P | M |

Answer [   ]

3 | J | K | L | J | K | L | M | N | O | | M | N | O | P | Q |

Answer [   ]

4 | K | L | M | K | L | N | K | L | | M | N | O | K | P |

Answer [   ]

5 | A | B | L | M | N | A | B | O | P | | R | S | M | N | Q |

Answer [   ]

6 | A | B | C | V | A | B | C | W | A | B | C | X | | A | B | C | Y | Z |

Answer [   ]

7 | M | N | O | P | Q | O | R | S | O | T | U | O | | T | V | W | X | Y |

Answer [   ]

8 | q | p | o | q | p | o | q | p | o | q | p | o | | o | p | r | s | q |

Answer [   ]

9 | U | V | V | W | X | X | Y | Z | | Z | V | W | X | Y |

Answer [   ]

10 | h | t | u | q | r | s | h | t | u | | s | u | t | q | h |

Answer [   ]

		1	**2**	**3**	**4**	**5**

11 | a | b | d | e | g | h | j | k | | l | m | n | o | p |

Answer [ ]

12 | K | L | M | M | N | O | P | P | | Q | R | S | T | U |

Answer [ ]

13 | A | V | W | B | X | Y | C | | A | X | Y | Z | V |

Answer [ ]

14 | p | p | r | r | t | t | v | v | | x | y | z | v | a |

Answer [ ]

15 | I | I | I | H | H | G | F | F | F | E | | G | H | E | F | D |

Answer [ ]

16 | C | D | C | D | A | B | E | F | E | F | A | B | | K | G | H | I | J |

Answer [ ]

17 | I | J | J | K | K | K | L | L | L | | O | K | N | L | M |

Answer [ ]

18 | R | Q | P | O | | M | O | P | L | N |

Answer [ ]

19 | J | K | L | S | T | M | N | O | S | T | | Q | P | R | S | T |

Answer [ ]

20 | o | q | s | u | | v | t | o | w | x |

Answer [ ]

	1	**2**	**3**	**4**	**5**

21 | r | s | t | r | s | t | u | r | s | t | u | v | | t | s | r | x | w |

Answer [ ]

22 | r | s | r | t | u | t | v | w | v | x | y | | y | x | z | w | t |

Answer [ ]

23 | W | W | X | W | X | Y | Y | Z | Y | | Y | X | Z | W | V |

Answer [ ]

24 | N | X | O | P | X | Q | R | S | X | | S | T | U | V | Q |

Answer [ ]

25 | a | c | f | j | | p | o | n | m | r |

Answer [ ]

26 | K | L | N | O | R | S | | W | X | V | U | T |

Answer [ ]

27 | m | p | n | q | o | r | p | | t | u | v | r | s |

Answer [ ]

28 | o | u | p | v | q | | v | p | w | x | y |

Answer [ ]

29 | E | H | L | O | S | | W | X | Y | V | Z |

Answer [ ]

30 | C | D | E | F | G | I | J | K | L | N | O | P | | R | S | T | U | V |

Answer [ ]

1 2 3 4 5

31 | D | G | I | L | N | | P | Q | R | S | T |

Answer | |

32 | k | p | u | l | q | | u | v | w | t | x |

Answer | |

33 | u | a | r | d | o | | f | h | g | k | l |

Answer | |

34 | A | L | M | B | P | Q | C | | R | S | U | T | V |

Answer | |

35 | A | B | X | C | D | Y | E | F | | Y | W | H | G | Z |

Answer | |

36 | Q | W | P | X | O | Y | N | | Z | X | R | S | T |

Answer | |

Quantitative relations tests

Usually in this test you are given a table of three rows and three columns of numbers. In each row there is a numerical relationship, which is the same for all the rows in the same table. Your task is to work out this numerical relationship and to replace the question mark in one of the rows with an appropriate number, using the other two rows as your guide. You do this by choosing one of the four answers provided, as illustrated in the example below.

X	Y	Z
19	7	24
33	15	36
12.8	5.3	?

A	B	C	D
12	15	16	17

The relationship within each row is:

$$X - Y = Z/2$$

First row: $19 - 7 = 24/2 = 12$
Second row: $33 - 15 = 36/2 = 18$
Third row: $12.8 - 5.3 = 15/2 = 7.5$

Therefore you should select B (15) as your answer to replace the question mark.

Tips

● I suggest that you first attempt to take this test within the given time limit, then go to the end of the chapter; where you will find the answers. Scrutinize all the numerical relationships thoroughly for every question and understand how they are formed. If you feel confident that you have understood all the different numerical relationship possibilities, then take the test again and compare your result with the first attempt and see the difference.

● This test deals with basic principles of numerical relationship, so the ability to use quick mental arithmetic could save you valuable time during the actual test. Again, I recommend that you read the tips on numerical estimation tests in Chapter 5 to help you to develop quick mental arithmetic skills.

Now try the following test, which consists of 32 questions that must be answered within a time limit of 16 minutes.

1

X	Y	Z
69	15	54
30	?	28
13	2	11

A	B	C	D
2	3	4	6

Answer [   ]

2

X	Y	Z
84	9	?
72	37	218
60	15	150

A	B	C	D
106	166	176	186

Answer [   ]

3

X	Y	Z
?	4	6
35	19	8
92	38	27

A	B	C	D
20	16	12	14

Answer [   ]

4

X	Y	Z
12	9	?
11	33	66
8	3	27

A	B	C	D
35	40	45	55

Answer [   ]

5

X	Y	Z
27	16	43
18	70	88
66	?	96

A	B	C	D
25	40	35	30

Answer [   ]

6

X	Y	Z
4	9	45
5	11	66
5	?	18

A	B	C	D
2	4	3	9

Answer [   ]

7

X	Y	Z
55	5	12
84	12	?
46	2	24

A	B	C	D
6	8	12	16

Answer [   ]

8

X	Y	Z
80	32	1280
14	12	?
41	4	82

A	B	C	D
84	74	94	14

Answer [   ]

9

X	Y	Z
15	12	181
8	33	265
?	29	204

A	B	C	D
7	9	13	11

Answer [   ]

10

X	Y	Z
?	5	47
19	2	35
8	12	93

A	B	C	D
12	10	42	7

Answer [   ]

11

X	Y	Z
20	?	30
15	3	16
42	18	58

A	B	C	D
22	40	12	10

Answer [   ]

12

X	Y	Z
5	28	19
1	?	10
3	92	49

A	B	C	D
32	22	16	18

Answer [   ]

13

X	Y	Z
1	6	10
9	70	82
?	0	27

A	B	C	D
19	29	24	27

Answer [   ]

14

X	Y	Z
3	80	23
2	28	9
57	?	77

A	B	C	D
90	80	70	60

Answer [   ]

15

X	Y	Z
2	14	?
1	10	6
15	30	30

A	B	C	D
9	5	11	13

Answer [   ]

16

X	Y	Z
?	10	28
6	15	36
3	3	9

A	B	C	D
12	18	9	8

Answer [   ]

17

X	Y	Z
27	15	12
25	?	19
92	12	80

A	B	C	D
8	17	13	6

Answer [   ]

18

X	Y	Z
42	5	9
30	2	8
?	1	4

A	B	C	D
15	20	10	25

Answer [   ]

19

X	Y	Z
?	8	7
88	11	19
73	13	12

A	B	C	D
43	41	33	31

Answer [   ]

20

X	Y	Z
42	81	3
20	29	?
15	11	19

A	B	C	D
9	11	17	23

Answer [   ]

21

X	Y	Z
15	2	3
10	?	17
22	4	14

A	B	C	D
7	5	3	9

Answer [   ]

22

X	Y	Z
21	3	6
63	9	?
81	27	18

A	B	C	D
27	8	21	18

Answer [   ]

23

X	Y	Z
11	8	80
10	7	63
?	13	13

A	B	C	D
1	2	4	6

Answer [   ]

24

X	Y	Z
3.5	1.2	2.3
9.6	?	7.4
33.8	12.5	21.3

A	B	C	D
4.2	2.4	3.3	2.2

Answer [   ]

25

X	Y	Z
6.4	0.9	6.5
6.8	1.6	6.2
?	7.2	8

A	B	C	D
14.2	16.4	18.6	15

Answer [   ]

26

X	Y	Z
11	13.1	?
40	2.5	22.5
19	3.4	12.9

A	B	C	D
20.4	18.6	11.6	16.8

Answer [   ]

27

X	Y	Z
2.3	6.9	2.3
2.5	18.5	?
7.4	23.2	7.9

A	B	C	D
8.2	8	7.8	6.9

Answer [   ]

28

X	Y	Z
3.3	9.9	11.6
1.2	2.8	6.6
1.4	?	11

A	B	C	D
5.8	6.4	7.4	8.6

Answer [   ]

29

X	Y	Z
?	9.9	3.3
5	21.2	5.3
9	32.8	4.1

A	B	C	D
7	8.4	6.2	4

Answer [   ]

30

X	Y	Z
2	26.4	6.6
6	13.6	1.7
?	10.8	2.7

A	B	C	D
6.1	5.3	4	2

Answer [   ]

31

X	Y	Z
6.7	21	17.3
3.4	37	36.6
8.4	17	?

A	B	C	D
11.6	12.3	9.6	6.11

Answer [   ]

32

X	Y	Z
89.9	10.9	70
75.4	14.4	?
13.2	2.5	1.7

A	B	C	D
50	52	49.3	41.4

Answer [   ]

Logical patterns and sequences

This is the ability to think strictly logically in abstract terms. In this test you are given a row of four figures on the left-hand side of the page and four figures on the right hand side. The four figures on the left contain several symbols, patterned in a logical sequence, and you are asked to discover how the sequence is constructed and how it works. When you have found that, you have to complete the logical sequence with one and only one figure from the right hand side of the page on the same row. Look at the example below.

Example 1

The answer is B, as there have to be 5 lines in the square. (1st square 1 line, 2nd square 2 lines, 3rd square 3 lines, and so on).

Example 2

The answer is B, as the triangle movement is 90 degrees anti-clockwise. The next or fifth position would thus be pointing upward.

Example 3

The answer is A. The stars form alternate diagonals.

When you are ready and confident that you have understood the concept, try the 25 questions and allow yourself five minutes to finish.

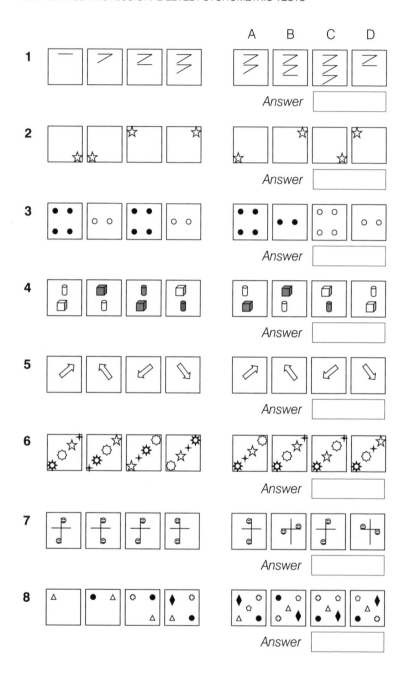

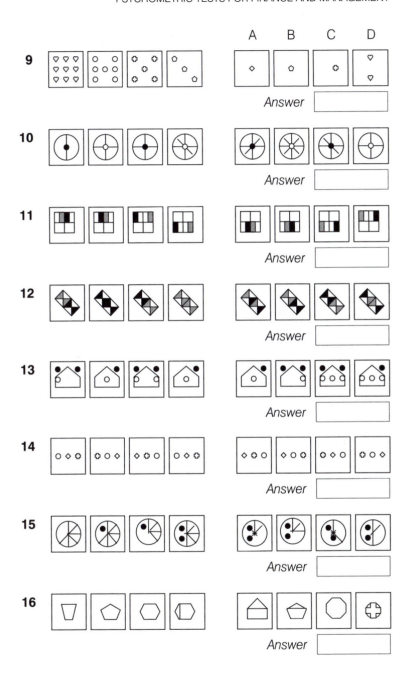

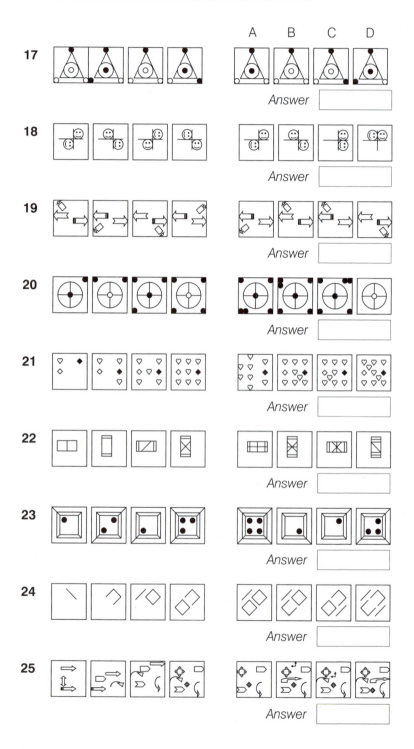

Account checking

Accuracy is an essential skill required in many financial and management roles. As figures can make or break a company, the ability to scrutinize numbers for accuracy and to find mistakes is essential in many jobs that require entering data into a computer, checking tables and accounts, calculating balances, making an order for replenishing stock in a warehouse or a supermarket, etc.

This test consists of two forms of written information. On the first page you have the original cards of 10 customers' balances and on the next page there is a table showing the computer-produced printout displaying all the accounts. Your task is to check and compare the original cards of balances against the computer printout and decide whether the computer printout has displayed the information accurately.

Tips

Skim through the cards quickly and identify key points from each card. Try to build a table in your memory by differentiating cards with debit and others with credit, for example. You could choose another method, according to your ability and skills in memorizing, to answer the questions quickly and accurately.

In the test, each line of the computer printout has been numbered, as shown in the table. If there are any errors in the computer printout mark the line and the corresponding columns, ie A, B, C, D, E and F where each error occurred. If there are no errors in that question, mark G. In a real test you will be provided with a separate answer sheet to mark your answers.

You have five minutes to attempt as many of the 20 questions as you can.

1
A	Name:	Bill Davies
B	Acc No:	40044390
C	Type of Acc:	Deposit
D	Date	9 Oct 06
E	Balance:	£890.90
F	Debit	☐

6
A	Name:	Martin Green
B	Acc No:	506744777
C	Type of Acc:	Deposit
D	Date	1 July 07
E	Balance:	£860.90
F	Credit	☐

2
A	Name:	Hiten Patel
B	Acc No:	79844395
C	Type of Acc:	Current
D	Date	5 March 04
E	Balance:	£90.90
F	Credit	☐

7
A	Name:	Kiran Parshad
B	Acc No:	35444390
C	Type of Acc:	Deposit
D	Date	10 Oct 06
E	Balance:	£1,000.00
F	Debit	☐

3
A	Name:	Nikki Brown
B	Acc No:	92443570
C	Type of Acc:	Deposit
D	Date	9 Sept 05
E	Balance:	£5,678.00
F	Credit	☐

8
A	Name:	Rabie Dean
B	Acc No:	65647379
C	Type of Acc:	Current
D	Date	9 Nov 02
E	Balance:	£2,134.00
F	Debit	☐

4
A	Name:	Paula Woods
B	Acc No:	44567892
C	Type of Acc:	e-Saver
D	Date	13 April 01
E	Balance:	£12,578.00
F	Credit	☐

9
A	Name:	Zufi Muhad
B	Acc No:	73217898
C	Type of Acc:	Deposit
D	Date	23 June 03
E	Balance:	£27,456.00
F	Credit	☐

5
A	Name:	Daniel Brown
B	Acc No:	40044390
C	Type of Acc:	Current
D	Date	21 May 02
E	Balance:	£17,834.00
F	Credit	☐

10
A	Name:	Gary Grimme
B	Acc No:	40044390
C	Type of Acc:	e-Saver
D	Date	9 Aug 08
E	Balance:	£18,744.00
F	Debit	☐

Printout by computer

	Name	Acc No.	Type of account	Date	Balance	Credit /Debit	NO Error
	A	B	C	D	E	F	G
1	Bill Davies	40044890	Deposit	9 Oct 06	£890.98	Debit	
2	Kiran Parshad	35444390	Deposit	10 Oct 02	£10000.00	Debit	
3	Nikki Brown	92443570	Current	9 Sep 05	£5678.00	Debit	
4	Rabie Dean	65647379	Current	9 Nov 02	£2143.00	Debit	
5	Paula Woods	44567892	e-Saver	13 April 01	£12587.00	Credit	
6	Zufi Muhad	73217898	Deposit	23 June 03	£27456.00	Credit	
7	Daniel Brown	40044390	Current	21 May 04	£17834.00	Debit	
8	Gary Grimme	40044390	e-Saver	9 Aug 08	£18744.00	Debit	
9	Martin Green	506644777	Deposit	1 July 02	£860.90	Credit	
10	Hiten Patel	79844395	Deposit	5 March 04	£90.90	Debit	
11	Nikki Brown	92443570	Deposit	9 Sep 08	£5678.00	Credit	
12	Paula Woods	44567892	e-Saver	13 April 01	£12578.00	Credit	
13	Kiran Parshad	35444390	Deposit	10 Oct 02	£100.00	Debit	
14	Bill Davies	40044390	Deposit	9 Oct 06	£809.09	Credit	
15	Rabie Dean	65467379	Current	9 Nov 02	£2134.00	Credit	
16	Hiten Patel	79899395	Current	5 March 07	£90.90	Credit	
17	Zufi Muhad	73217898	Deposit	23 June 03	£27456.00	Credit	
18	Martin Green	506744777	Current	1 July 07	£890.90	Credit	
19	Gary Grimme	48844390	e-Saver	6 Aug 02	£18744.00	Debit	
20	Daniel Brown	40044390	Current	21 May 02	£17834.00	Debit	

Table checking

Usually very little time is allowed in tests of this kind: between 8 and 15 seconds per question, depending on the test and the company providing the test. Therefore, it is important to work quickly and accurately. There are many ways this test can be presented. What is given here is a flavour of what you may get in your actual test, and I leave it to your creativity to design further examples and set the time limit to meet your ability. However, I will mention here, briefly, a few examples from the popular formats.

Example 1

Identifying the identical pair from among many columns:

A	B	C	D	E
XYZ232	XYZ332	XYZ234	XYZ232	XZY232

Here there is only one identical pair, in columns A and D.

The test could be presented in the form of an original set of items, ie a string of characters, symbols, etc, to compare with a typed copy that differs from the original, organized in single columns; you have to pinpoint the differences.

Example 2

Finding symbols that differ from the original:

Original	Typed Copy
A B C D 5 E 6 F 7 G 8 H 9	A B C D 5 6 F 7 G 8 H 9

As you can see, the character E in the original is missing in the typed copy.

In another form you would have to compare the first column string of letters and numbers with a number of copies in different columns and again mark the mistakes in each column, as shown below.

Example 3

Same format as example 2 but using multiple columns.

Original	Copy 1	Copy 2	Copy 3	Copy 4
X Y Z % T &	Z % T &	X Y Z &	X Y Z % T &	X Y % T &

As you can see, XY is missing in the Copy 1 column, and % and T are missing from the Copy 2 column. There are no mistakes in the Copy 3 column, and Z is missing from the Copy 4 column.

Example 4

Another type involves comparing sets of characters or symbols arranged in pairs, one on the left and another on the right, and pinpointing how many pairs are identical in a single question:

ILOVE	ILOV
SD&M7	SD&M7
ROTOR	ROTOR

In this example, two of the three given pairs are identical.

Next there are two tests using the formats in example 1 and example 2.

Example 1 test – Identifying the identical pair from among many columns

Tips

My advice is to take four or five letters or numbers (depending on your ability) from the first or last column and compare them with the rest. When you find the matches compare the remaining character(s). The choice of four letters is optional and could be from any column (see the diagram).

Finally compare the remaining letters

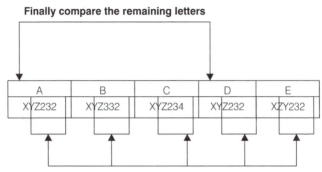

**First compare only 4 characters from column A with the rest
When you find a match compare the remainder of column A
with the column(s) that match(es) the first four characters**

When you are ready and confident that you have understood the concept, try the test below and allow yourself eight minutes to finish. Mark the two identical sets of characters using the letters of the of the appropriate columns (A, B, C, D, E or F) on a separate answer sheet.

	A	B	C	D	E	F
1.	XNM23%	XNL23%	MXN23%	NXM23%	XNM32%	XNM23%
2.	1*$2RTY	12*$RTY	1*2$RTY	1*2$RYT	1*2$RTY	1*2R$TY
3.	OPQ65K	OPQ56K	OQP56K	OPQ56K	QOP56K	KOPQ56
4.	XCVBN	XCVBN	XCBVN	XCVNB	XVCBN	XCBNV
5.	LNM$*W	LNM*$W	MN*$WL	LMN*$W	LMN$*W	LMN*$W
6.	GHI49!	HGI4=9!	GHI4=9!	GHI4=!9	GHI4=9!	GHI=49!
7.	TRE&R%	TRER&%	TER&R%	TRE %	TRE&R%	TR&ER%
8.	DCE?R*	CDE?R*	CDE?R*	CDE? *R	CED?R*	CDER*?
9.	TIR6532	IRT6532	ITR5632	ITR6523	ITR6532	ITR6532
10.	JQ&W80$	JQW&80$	JQW&08$	JQW&80$	JQW&8$0	QJW&80$
11.	A*D65&	A*D6&5	A*D65&	A*D56&	A D *65&	A*65 D &
12.	#4T&(R*	#4T&R(*	#4TR& (*	4#&R(*	#4T&R(*	4#T& (*
13.	8Q5TH?	QT85H?	Q85T?H	Q85TH?	Q58TH?	Q85TH?
14.	2 M ^ $5K	M2 ^ $ K 5	M2 ^ 5$K	M2 ^ $5K	M2 ^ $5K	M ^ 2$5K
15.	OLO4K%	OLKO4%	OLKO4%	OLOK4%	OLK40%	LOKO4%

	A	B	C	D	E	F
16.	VW8$42	WV48$2	VW4$82	VW48$2	VW48$2	WV482$
17.	TRL9#%	TRL9%#	TRL9#%	RTL9#%	TR9#L%	TR9L%#
18.	KL4&#W	KL4#&W	K4L&#W	KL4&#W	KWL4&#	L4K&#W
19.	POI7834	PIO7834	PO7I834	POI7483	POI7384	POI7834
20.	?3ERNV	?83ERVN	?83ENRV	?8E3RNV	?83ERVN	?8ERNV
21.	FLE9@4	LEF9@4	LFE9@4	LF9E@4	LFE94@	LFE9@4
22.	OTR731	OTR71	OT731	OR731	OTR731	ORT71
23.	OP?\24%	PO?\24%	OP\?24%	OP?2\4%	OP?\24	OP?\24%
24.	XC8*L?3	X8*L?3	X8C*L?3	XC8L*?3	XC8*L3?	XC8*L?3
25.	MN$%L9	MN$%L9	MN%L9	ML N%$9	NM$%9	MN$%L9
26.	56P78H$	56P78$H	56P87H$	5P678H$	56P78H$	65P78H$
27.	%M&7*T	%M7&*T	M7% &*T	%M7*T&	%M7&*T	%M7&T *
28.	#OYT%	#YT*%	#0YT*%	#OYT*%	#0T*%	OYT*%
29.	PTR68!	PR68!	TPR68!	PTR86!	PTR68!	TRP68!
30.	TR6&231	TR6&321	TR63&21	TR6&321	TR&621	TR6&31
31.	E4R5T6G	4ER5T6G	E4R56GT	E4RT56G	E4R5T6G	EG4R5T6
32.	O15REW	OT4REW	OT5RWE	OT5REW	OT5REW	OT5RFW
33.	IT&D*$	IT&D*$	IT&D$*	T1&D*$	IT&D$	ITD*$
34.	LKD579	L5KD97	LK5D97	LDK597	LKD597	LKD597
35.	QSA&$T	QAS&$T	QAS&$T	QAS&T$	QAS$T	QA&$T
36.	9RT67	69RT67	69R67	6RT67	69RT67	6RT76
37.	JDSETI4	JDSTI4	JSETI4	JDSET4	JDSETI	JDSETI4
38.	M56&$	N56$	NM56$&	NM6&$	NM56&$	NM56&$
39.	JTRLNOP	JTLNOP	JTRLNOP	JRLNOP	TRLNOP	JTRLNP
40.	139587&	1-39587&	1-3587&	1-3957&	1-3958&	1-39587&
41.	985HTR4	985TR4	985HTR4	85HTR4	95HTR4	985T4R
42.	TR24&*	TR47&*	T247&*	TR247&*	TR247&*	TR247&
43.	QR%8H	Q%#8H	QR%#8H	QR%#8H	QR#8H	QR%#8
44.	TJKLMN	TKJLMN	TJKMLN	TJLKMN	NJKLMT	TJLKMN
45.	Y6H78HY	YH768HY	YH678HY	YH678HY	YH678YH	YH687HY

Example 2 test – Finding symbols that differ from the original

In this test you are presented with a copy of the original symbols. You are required to cross out the symbols in the copy that differ from those in the original. Usually very little time is given in these tests, so it is important to work quickly and efficiently. Try this test and allow yourself eight minutes to finish.

	Original								Copy							
									A	B	C	D	E	F	G	H
1	Š	<	⚲	ᴧᴧ	¢	↔	Ӂ	#	Š	<	⚳	ᴧᴧ	∞	↔	Ӂ	#
2	@	П	\	ж	¤	Ц	Ц	♍	@	П	/	ж	Ô	Ц	⚳	♍
3	⬩	♛	℀	Ψ	♈	♋	≈	⊕	⬩	♛	℀	♈	♈	♋	≈	⊕
4	vii	△	∅	↡	∉	⤸	∨	⌂	vii	▷	∅	↡	∉	⤸	∨	∅
5	✝	♋	♂	▧	✒	☒	☢	☠	⊤	♋	♭	▧	✒	☒	⊕	☠
6	☦	★	☛	☃	⚓	☁	☀	☆	☦	✳	☛	☃	☂	⌂	☀	☆
7	☿	♜	✈	✉	C	✐	✤	♪	☿	♜	⬩	✉	C	✐	♣	♪
8	⚶	✿	❄	✳	☀	❥	¶	❖	✝	✿	❄	✳	☀	❥	¶	✡
9	♪	<	>	⊤	❖	☁	☂	♌	♪	>	>	⊤	☀	☁	¶	♌
10	❣	⚡	⤸	⑧	⇨	→✳	✳	❅	❣	⚡	✦	⑧	⇨	✳	✳	❅
11	Q	➵	U	≻	♍	⊤	₩	Ⱦ	∅	➵	U	∋	♍	⊤	♍	Ⱦ
12	§	Đ	õ	Ũ	ʧ	б	ш	ᶎ	§	Ď	õ	Ũ	ʧ	Ŏ	ш	ᶎ
13	Т	₩	R	Oy	V̌	Й	ʊ	℥	Т	₩	K	Oy	Ñ	Й	ʊ	℥
14	♪	F	↑	Ю	Ö	◡	Ɉ	ᷡ	‼	F	↑	Ю	Ö	◡	J	ᷡ
15	%	Ë	»»	Ğ	V	⊤	DŽ	Ă	%	Ë	»»	Ě	V	⊤	DŽ	Ë
16	ћ	S	J	ᶾ	æ	Æ	ω	Ⱶ	ћ	S	L	ᶾ	æ	Æ	щ	Ⱶ
17	ою	฿	⚹	℮	Ğ	Ч	D	☝	ою	฿	⚹	ʠ	Ğ	Y	D	☝
18	⚌	K	⚍	✕	☥	☺	☾	●	⚌	K	⚍	ж	☺	☺	☽	●
19	✛	ℭ	⚰	☥	‡	☯	↗	♚	✛	ℭ	☽	☥	‡	☀	↗	♞
20	Ψ	♙	✖	☆	✝	✳	✳	✳	Ψ	♙	✖	♙	✝	✳	☆	✳

	Original								Copy A	B	C	D	E	F	G	H
21	⇛	ⓓ	ȣ	N	☩	K	⊠	⌒	⇛	ⓓ	ㄆ	N	☩	K	⊠	⌒
22	Z	◆	π	ڡ	Ỷ	8	Ĉ	Ę	Z	◆	π	ڡ	Ỷ	8	C	Ę
23	M	✳	♛	Ż	ҕ	Π	Ψ	Ӟ	M	✳	♛	Ż	ҕ	Π	Ψ	Ŏ
24	℧	L	⅄	ε	9	7	¢	¤	℧	L	⅄	Ɛ	9	7	φ	¤
25	Б	5	K	ڡ	Ξ	Σ	Ψ	Ω	Б	6	K	ڡ	Ξ	Ʒ	Ψ	Ω
26	ὼ	3	ҕ	ы	ю	ж	Љ	Њ	Ѵ	3	ҕ	ы	Ю	ж	Љ	Њ
27	G	Ø	ï	ij	Ŧ	ŧ	NJ	Ӝ	G	Ø	ï	ij	Ŧ	ŧ	NL	Ӝ
28	ⱷ	⋈	Y	F	8	ⱻ	∊	⋙	ⱷ	⋰	Y	F	8	⊑	∊	⋙
29	⩔	2	⊗	⌧	⌘	⊡	⊤	9	⩔	2	⊗	⌧	%	⊡	⊤	8
30	♪	Ч	G	8	⏛	‖▪	①↔	ʄ	ʅ	Ч	G	8	⏛	‖▪	①↔	⨎
31	£	Ɠ	⇐	⊐	⨴	Đ	xi	⇆	£	Ɠ	⇒	⊐	⨴	Đ	xi	⇄
32	↺	←	↑	↞	↦	⥮	↕	⇜	↺	←	↑	↞	↦	↕	⥮	⇜
33	⇐	⇑	⇒	⇓	⇑	⥯	⥮	⇥	⇐	⇑	⇒	⇑	⇑	⥯	⥮	↤
34	↳	↰	↵	⌒	⌒	⬉	⇻	⇼	↳	↱	↵	⌒	⌒	⬉	⇻	⇺
35	⇄	⇅	⇅	⇆	⇇	⇈	⇄	⇊	⇄	⇅	⇅	⇆	⇇	⇊	⇄	⇈
36	⇑	⇒	⇓	⇔	⇕	⬉	⬀	⬊	⇑	⇒	⇓	⇐	⇑	⬉	⬀	⬊
37	i	ii	iii	iv	v	vi	vii	viii	i	ii	iv	iv	v	iii	vii	viii
38	v	vi	vii	vii	viii	ix	x	xi	v	vi	vii	xii	viii	ix	v	xi
39	∫	∬	∭	⨍	⨎	⨙	⨍	⨍	∫	∭	∬	⨍	⨎	⨙	⨍	⨍
40	≈	≈	≠	≅	≇	≢	≈	≠	≏	≈	≠	≅	≇	≢	≍	≠
41	≤	≥	≦	≧	⪋	⪌	≪	≫	≤	≥	≦	≧	⪌	⪋	≪	≫
42	⊂	⊃	⊄	⊅	⊆	⊇	⊈	⊉	⊃	⊂	⊄	⊅	⊆	⊇	⊈	⊉
43	⊏	⊐	⊑	⊒	⊓	⊔	∩	∪	⊏	⊐	⊈	⊉	⊓	⊔	∩	∪
44	⊢	⊣	⊤	⊥	⊦	⊧	⊨	⊩	⊢	⊣	⊤	⊥	⊦	⊧	⊨	⊩
45	↘	⇢	↗	↘	↣	↗	↦	⇒	↘	⇢	↗	↘	➡	↗	↦	⇒

Answers for Chapter 2

Number series

1	B	+6
2	A	×2
3	C	−3
4	D	÷3
5	A	+0.6
6	A	×2
7	D	+1, +2, +3, +4, +5
8	C	−7, −6, −5, −4, −3
9	B	Add two previous numbers: 29+19=48, 48+67=115
10	C	Multiply two previous numbers: 2×5=10, 5×10=50
11	D	Power of 2: 2^2, 2^3, 2^4, 2^5, 2^6
12	A	×1, ×2, ×3, ×4
13	C	−3, −2, −1, 0
14	D	÷4, ÷3, ÷2, ÷1
15	A	−5+1, −4+1, −3+1
16	A	+1, −2, +3, −4, +5
17	D	−1, +2, −3, +4, −5, +6
18	D	×2, +2, ×2, +2
19	B	+2, ×3, +2, ×3
20	C	−3, ×3, −3, ×3
21	A	+4 −3 ×3, +4 −3 ×3, +4
22	B	×3 ÷2 +2, ×3 ÷2 +2 ×3
23	D	×4 −1, ×4 −1, ×4
24	C	+4 +3 −2, +4 +3 −2, +4
25	B	×4 ÷2, ×4 ÷4, ×4÷2, ×4÷4
26	C	÷5 ×5 +5, ÷5 ×5 +5 ÷5
27	B	×2 +2 ÷2, ×2 +2 ÷2
28	A	÷2 ×4, ÷2 ×4, ÷2 ×4
29	D	+5 ×2, +5 ×2, +5

30 D $\times 3, \times 1, \times 6, \times 1, \times 9$

31 A Hope series: 1st series (1, 3, 7, 13),
2nd series (1, 3, 9, 27)

32 D Hope series: 1st series (9, 6, 3, 0),
2nd series (1.5, 3, 6, 12)

33 C The cubes numbers: $1^3, 2^3, 3^3, 4^3, 5^3$

34 A Alternative sign $\times 3$

35 C $\times 2 -5, \times 2 -5, \times 2 -5$

36 A Subtract two previous numbers: 67–13=54, 87–26=61

37 A Hope series: 1st series (81, 9, 1, 0.11),
2nd series (0.5, 0.75, 1)

38 B $-1 +2, -3 +4, -5 +6, -7 +8$

39 C Mirror pattern

40 A Add two previous numbers: 79+8=87, 87+95=182

Character series

1	3	**10**	4	**19**	2	**28**	3
2	3	**11**	2	**20**	4	**29**	4
3	1	**12**	1	**21**	3	**30**	1
4	4	**13**	4	**22**	2	**31**	2
5	5	**14**	1	**23**	3	**32**	2
6	1	**15**	3	**24**	2	**33**	3
7	2	**16**	2	**25**	2	**34**	4
8	5	**17**	4	**26**	1	**35**	5
9	1	**18**	5	**27**	5	**36**	1

Quantitative relations tests

1	A	$X - Y = Z$		**17**	D	$Z + Y = X$
2	D	$X + Y = Z/2$		**18**	A	$Z + Y = X/3$
3	B	$X - Y = 2Z$		**19**	A	$Z + Y = (X + 2)/3$
4	C	$Z - Y = 3X$		**20**	B	$Z + Y = 2X$
5	D	$X + Y = Z$		**21**	C	$Z + X = Y \times 9$
6	C	$Z/Y = X + 1$		**22**	D	$X - Y = 3Z$
7	B	$X/Y = Z - 1$		**23**	B	$Z/Y = X - 1$
8	A	$X \times Y = 2Z$		**24**	D	$X - Y = Z$
9	A	$X \times Y = Z - 1$		**25**	A	$X - Y = Z - 1$
10	B	$X \times Y = Z + 3$		**26**	B	$Z - Y = X/2$
11	C	$Z - Y = X - 2$		**27**	B	$Y - X = 2Z$
12	D	$Z - X = Y/2$		**28**	C	$Y - X = Z - 5$
13	C	$Z - X = Y + 3$		**29**	D	$Y/Z = X - 1$
14	B	$Z - X = Y/4$		**30**	D	$Y/Z = X + 2$
15	A	$Z - X = Y/2$		**31**	A	$X + Z = Y + 3$
16	D	$Z - X = Y \times 2$		**32**	B	$X - Y = Z + 9$

Logical patterns and sequences

1	B	**8**	D	**15**	B	**22**	C
2	C	**9**	A	**16**	C	**23**	B
3	A	**10**	C	**17**	B	**24**	A
4	D	**11**	A	**18**	A	**25**	B
5	A	**12**	B	**19**	B		
6	B	**13**	C	**20**	C		
7	C	**14**	D	**21**	D		

Account checking

1	B & E	8	G	15	B & F
2	D & E	9	B & D	16	B & D
3	C & F	10	C & F	17	G
4	E	11	D	18	C & E
5	E	12	G	19	B & D
6	B & C	13	D & E	20	F
7	D & F	14	E & F		

Table checking

Example 1 – Identifying the identical pair from among many columns

1	A & F	16	D & E	31	A & E
2	C & E	17	A & C	32	D & E
3	B & D	18	A & D	33	A & B
4	A & B	19	A & F	34	E & F
5	D & F	20	B & E	35	B & C
6	C & E	21	C & F	36	B & E
7	A & E	22	A & E	37	A & F
8	B & C	23	A & F	38	E & F
9	E & F	24	A & F	39	A & C
10	B & D	25	B & F	40	B & F
11	A & C	26	A & E	41	A & C
12	B & E	27	B & E	42	D & E
13	D & F	28	C & D	43	C & D
14	D & E	29	A & E	44	A & F
15	B & C	30	B & D	45	C & D

Example 2 – Finding symbols that differ from the original

1	C & E	**16**	C & G	**31**	C & H
2	C & E & G	**17**	D & F	**32**	A & B & H
3	A & D	**18**	D & E & G	**33**	D & H
4	B & H	**19**	C & F	**34**	B & H
5	A & C & G	**20**	D & G	**35**	F & H
6	B & F	**21**	A & C	**36**	D & E
7	C & G	**22**	C & G	**37**	C & F
8	A & D & H	**23**	B & H	**38**	D & G
9	B & E & G	**24**	D & G	**39**	B & C
10	C & F	**25**	B & F	**40**	A & G
11	A & D & G	**26**	A & E	**41**	E & F
12	B & F	**27**	C & G	**42**	A & B
13	C & E & H	**28**	B & F	**43**	C & D
14	A & G	**29**	E & H	**44**	G & H
15	D & H	**30**	A & H	**45**	B & E

Chapter 3
Psychometric tests for IT

High-level programming language tests

Owing to the shortage of well-qualified IT specialists, most companies nowadays recruit people from all walks of life. It is not necessary to have know-how or qualifications in IT subjects, only the desire and ability to think logically. Most industries offer intensive courses in different high-level programming languages eg, JAVA, C and Pascal, and it is a matter of time before you become an expert programmer.

High-level languages are geared towards the people writing the program rather than the computer. These languages provide the interface between the user and the machine. They are as close to English as you can get and are easy to program since their operations closely resemble the language in which the problem is formulated, rather than the internal computer architecture. However, they are sufficiently scrupulous to allow the computer to translate the program written in the high-level language into machine language. This translation is accomplished by means of a special computer program called a 'compiler'. Since each computer system has its own machine language, a different compiler is required for each different high-level language. The compiler checks your program for errors. If there are errors, the compiler issues an error message or warning. The compiler checks for a variety of errors, some of which are used as practice exercises in this test. It is not unusual to have to compile your program many times until all errors have been deleted from the program.

In this book I present two kinds of compiler checking. For this exercise you will play the role of compiler to identify the errors in the mock-up programs described below. If you already have some programming skills, be careful not to confuse yourself, because the programs here don't abide by the usual programming rules used in high-level language. Also, be aware that you will have *no* time to compile your program more than once, owing to the tight time set for the test. Therefore, you need to pinpoint errors first time and to work quickly and accurately.

Compiler checking by tracking error

In this test you will find a mock-up of unstructured programming lines, taken from a 'C' lookalike language, which contain many errors. The errors have been identified and categorized into three types: syntax error (SE), logical error (LE) and other error (OE). Each of the three types of errors has its own set of rules. Using these rules, your task is to trace and determine the exact location of an error in each programming line and then identify what type of error its, ie SE, LE or OE. If no rule has been broken, cross the column 'no error' (NE).

Look at the following example:

		SE	LE	OE	NE
1.	Printf ("\n Maximum and minimum of the 3 numbers				

Now look at the set of rules in Figure 3.1.

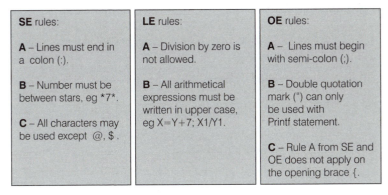

SE rules:

A – Lines must end in a colon (:).

B – Number must be between stars, eg *7*.

C – All characters may be used except @, $.

LE rules:

A – Division by zero is not allowed.

B – All arithmetical expressions must be written in upper case, eg X=Y+7; X1/Y1.

OE rules:

A – Lines must begin with semi-colon (;).

B – Double quotation mark (") can only be used with Printf statement.

C – Rule A from SE and OE does not apply on the opening brace {.

FIGURE 3.1   SE, LE and OE rules

As you can see, rules A and B in SE have been broken; the line should end in a colon and the number, ie 3, should be between stars. No rules are broken in LE. Rule A has been broken in OE, because of the missing semi-colon at the beginning of the line. Therefore, you should cross the SE and OE columns, like this:

		SE	LE	OE	NE
1.	Printf ('\n Maximum and minimum of the 3 numbers	X		X	

Now try the following exercise. See how many you can complete in 10 minutes, then compare your results with the answers given at the end of this chapter.

		SE	LE	OE	NE
1	;Include<stdio.h>,				
2	;Include <math.h>:				
3	#define (NST):				
4	;double a1b1/x1, Y3				
5	;main (11Maxim@),				
6	;{				

		SE	LE	OE	NE
7	;Printf("na="); X/*0*=Y:				
8	;Scanf(7)%1f, &a):				
9	,Printf ("%f,*10*);X				
10	,(* Calculate ymax @ Ymax, "9"):				
11	XM=0.5+X2(Y1-Y2):				
12	;MAX=OR+T:				
13	;Printf("\n X=8%, Y=8%8+61),				
14	}				
15	;Void =X1/Y1+7				
16	{:				
17	;X1=A+0.5(B-A(NST):				
18	;Y1=x(R1):				
19	If (y1=y2) Then Y1=8+x				
20	Printf("n Interrst Rate");				
21	:For (c=1; c <=20/0;++ c);				
22	;L=0.01+n,				
23	,Return:				
24	,Scanf("a, @/B):				
25	;Maximum (x,y):				
26	;While (N/*0*=X+Y) Then X=Y:				
27	For (count=1; count<=n;count=1+n)				
28	,Func1(int n):				
29	;int y=X:				
30	;X/0=Y:				
31	;Return:				
32	}				
33	,Int Funct1 (inta1):				
34	;(int funct2 (X+Y=2)):				
35	,B=F($):				

		SE	LE	OE	NE
36	,Return;				
37	;/initialize and read in a value for /:				
38	; While x=y calculate the average :				
39	; AVERAGE=X+T–Y:				
40	;Read in the number:				
41	;For "(c=x; c<=n c=n+x)":				

Compiler checking by line rules

In this test you are presented with a mock-up programming language, designed to be similar to 'Pascal'. Here, however, the conditions are set for each individual line, rather than for the whole program as in the previous example. Your task is to discover which conditions, if any, have been broken. If more than one condition is broken, then you mark more than one column. If no conditions are broken, then mark column Z. Look at this example:

		W	X	Y	Z
A	Procedure Admittance (X=7:Real; VAR G, B:Real)				

Now look at the set of rules in Figure 3.2.

Conditions for line **A** in the program:	Conditions for line **B** in the program:	Conditions for line **C** in the program:
W – Lines must end in a *.	**W** – Lines must begin with the word Return.	**W** – All lines must start with an upper case letter.
X – Number must be between double quotation, eg "7".	**X** – All arithmetic expression must be written in Uppercase, eg X = Y + 2.	**X** – Double quotation mark (") cannot be used.
Y – All numbers may be used except 5 and 7.	**Y** – All characters may be used except @ and ?.	**Y** – Number must be between brackets eg (7) + (5).

FIGURE 3.2 Line rules

In the example the line is designated by the letter A, so you should look at Figure 3.2 and the conditions applied to line A. Rules W, X, Y have all been broken as there is no * at the end of the line; the number 7 should be between quotation marks; and number 7 should not have been used. Therefore, you should cross W, X and Y, like this:

		W	X	Y	Z
A	Procedure Admittance (X=7:Real; VAR G, B:Real)	X	X	X	

Now, try the following exercise. See how many you can complete in 10 minutes and compare your results with the answers given at the end of this chapter.

			W	**X**	**Y**	**Z**
1	A	Program A1 A2 A3 *				
2	B	Return ('Enter Vol Tages A1, A2, @, 5)				
3	C	If ABS(9) <0 AND ABS> "3"				
4	B	Return If no signal output then =X+y				
5	C	For N=0 to end points Do X=Y				
6	A	Procedure Traprule (B=7) *				
7	C	Return SUM=SUMY+X				
8	B	Retur N=Y+K,				
9	A	Area=SUMOF+H+ "4" +J				
10	B	Writeln (NI=5–X= ?)				
11	C	Trapezoidal =(2)+ "8"–(3)= 4;				
12	B	Return all prosedures to zero if possible?				
13	C	Var V1, V2, V4 are real,				
14	A	NO=(10–5)= "7"*				
15	C	Repeat x[M]=NO +(3)				
16	B	Array X[K] Until X=Y+1				
17	A	Function data "6" *				

			W	X	Y	Z
18	B	Return To the Upper class				
19	C	Procedures solution to all x=@+"1",				
20	A	' Newprogram="9"–"4"+X="5"X				
21	A	For K=I+1 to I–1 Do				
22	B	Reteren and then H–K=G+I				
23	C	Writeln Mean = 'SUM/N' – 8;				
24	A	Read(data) & SUM=X+Y*				
25	C	m=N*SUM/N (SUM)				
26	B	Return U=0+5+7				
27	A	X,Y: Array[1..3]{1..8},				
28	C	real array "8"+"3"				
29	B	Procedure Bestline Return*				
30	C	Read from (7) To (5)				
31	A	If Length < "15" then M=N*				
32	B	If Real AND Imaginary Equal Then X=Y				
33	C	return(All chartacter+Variables)				
34	B	While return Y+I=6				
35	A	Mean=K+T*				
36	B	Return=X=(9)+K is the total number*				
37	C	Const A1, 23, "9", ? and(X)				
38	A	If length >0 and N<8 then *				
39	B	While X=10 AND Y=20 Then				
40	A	Write x> "7" FOR ALL y<X				

Tip

This tip is based on testing a number of my students to see the best way to perform the test quickly and accurately. I found that taking all the programming lines in consecutive order is not a good way, because your brain has to keep switching back and forth between the rules for the three error types (SE, LE and OE) in compiler checking by tracking error, or the different lines (A, B or C) in compiler checking by line rules. This wastes time and leads to confusion. The best way is to handle one type of error at a time. Take for example the exercise for compiler checking by line rules. Instead of checking line after line, you simply take the conditions set for line A and test every line in the program where line A is identified, and mark your answer if the conditions are broken. When you have done this, look at the conditions for line B and, again, go through the whole program and test all lines marked B, and so on. In this way there are fewer rules to remember, you are less confused and your brain does not have to switch between conditions, so comparison is more accurate and fast. My students improved by about 70 per cent using this approach. However, practice brings mastery.

Assembly language test

Assembly language is a low-level language that is oriented towards the computer rather than the people who are programming it. To use a particular assembly language the programmer must have a thorough understanding of the internal architecture of the central processing unit (CPU) of that particular computer. The language consists of a list of instructions in mnemonic words and symbols. The number of instructions and commands used depends on the type of CPU, and they can only be executed on computers of identical design. Programming is very time-consuming to learn and it takes considerable experience to become proficient. Furthermore, programmers are always occupied with internal details of architecture rather than the actual program task to be accomplished. However, assembly language has a few advantages. First, it runs much faster than high-level language because it is nearer to the fundamental language (machine language, ie writing programs using a series of zeros and ones) for any computer. Second, there are some tasks that require direct access to hardware architecture that are more easily implemented by assembly language and may be difficult or impossible to do with high-level language.

Many IT companies are using the basic commands offered by assembly language to develop their own assembly language that is not related to any particular CPU architecture and is only used for testing candidates' computer aptitudes. Most of the commands and symbols used in these tests are simple if you have previous knowledge of assembly language programming; if not, such a test could be a very challenging experience. IT industries claim in their invitation letters that prior programming knowledge is not required, but it is difficult to comprehend how a candidate who has a degree in social science, has never programmed before and is interested in a career in the IT industry can understand the basic programming skills and answer the questions when attending these tests. Usually, no practice exercise is provided or sent to the candidates. During these tests you are given a manual to read and understand how the instructions of the given assembly language operate and a booklet with questions to answer. Usually the answers require you to write a simple program of between two and 12 lines. The test is designed to test your logical ability to read and understand material on a new programming language quickly, and to work under pressure to write as many programs as possible correctly.

In this section you will learn a few basic rules regarding lookalike assembly language programming. The important and most common elements are presented, which will be useful for inexperienced candidates. To familiarize yourself and minimize mistakes during your actual tests, read the provided examples, tests and solutions at the end of this chapter. See how the programs are written using different instructions. But don't forget in your actual test to follow the given instruction rules, which may differ from those in the examples given here.

Structure of assembly language

In the following test a number of fundamental characteristics, common to most assembly languages, will be introduced. We will use the following hypothetical microprocessor and associated assembly language, which contains the following basic elements:

- Six storage registers A_0, A, B, C, D and E. A_0 is used only as a temporary storage register, either to store the integer from the keyboard using the 'GetInt' instruction or to display its content on the screen using the 'ShoInt' instruction. A, B, C, D and E registers can be used to store variables, integers and constants. A full subset of the instruction set and their function operations used in this test are described in Table 3.1.

- The assembly language programs usually contain several passes of instructions; each one carries out a certain task. An example of an instruction and simple definitions using a single register A is:

  - Endfile: MOV A, 3   ;Data transfer, which means A = 3; Endfile: is called a label and is always separated by colon (:) and is written to the far left of an instruction. You can choose any name for your label. Labels are usually used in conjunction with branch instructions such as JMP, JMPZ, JMPE, JNE, JLO and JGO. Their operation function is described in Table 3.1.
  - MOV: is the instruction mnemonic. It means load or transfer the data from source (second operand) 3, to the destination (first operand), register A in the above example.

- Comments are always separated by a semicolon (;) and written to the far right of an instruction to explain the steps used to execute the program. Here they are used to help you annotate the program and understand the steps of execution. However, they are usually ignored during the actual tests, owing to the time limits.

- Important note: the source (second operand) could be any variable, integer, constant or a register, but the destination (first operand) must always be a register. Also, only one variable, integer or constant may be operated on at a given time, using a single register. So 3M, for example, consists of two variables 3 and M, which should be operated on or implemented separately.

TABLE 3.1   A full subset of the instruction set and their function operation used in this test

Mnemonic	Function	Result
MOV	MOV A, 2 MOV I,10	Load register A with 2, ie A=2 Allocate I=10
ADD	ADD A, 2 ADD A, B	Add 2 to register A content , ie A=A+2 Add A to B, ie A=A+B
SUB	SUB A, 2 SUB 2	Subtract 2 from register A content, ie A=A−2 Subtract the result in the last operation by 2
MUL	MUL A, 2	Multiply register A by 2, ie A=A×2
DIV	DIV A, 2	Divide register A by 2, ie A=A/2
INC	INC A	Increment register A by one, ie A=A+1
DEC	DEC A	Decrement register A by one, ie A=A−1
CMP	CMP A, B CMP 2	Compare the content of registers: A&B, ie A=B, A<B or A>B. Compare the result in the last operation with 2.
JMP	JMP	Causes an unconditional jump. It could be to a "Label"
JMPZ	JMPZ	Jump if the result of an arithmetic operation in the last operation is zero
JMPE	JMPE	Jump if the result in the last operation produces an equal number
JNE	JNE	Jump if the result in the last operation produces a negative number
JLO	JLO	Jump if in the last operation the first operand was less than the second operand
JGO	JGO	Jump if in the last operation the first operand was greater than the second operand
GetInt	GetInt	Get an integer from the keyboard and store it in register A_0.
ShoInt	ShoInt	Display the contents of register A_0 on the screen

Tips

As mentioned before, these tests tend to be easy if you have some programming skills. However, the examples below and the provided test-solutions are a very good start in familiarizing yourself. I cannot recommend any particular book to help you because most are written for specific CPU architecture; nevertheless, it may help you to look at one (it doesn't matter which) to see the extensive list of instructions.

In most of these tests you are required to perform simple mathematical operations including counting and looping, and to follow simple rules:

- Simplify algebraic expressions by performing the operations inside parentheses first and reduce a fraction to the lowest possible terms, ie the numerator and denominator have no common factors, before writing your program; 8/12 + 8/6= 24/12 = 2. This final result should be used in your program.

- Multiplication/division must be programmed first, then addition or subtraction.

- Usually, a single storage register is allowed to store only one operand at a time, so before performing any mathematical operation using the second operand, make sure which operand you should express first, for example:

  ADD A, B   ;A=A+B
  ADD B, A   ;B=B+A

- Usually the instruction 'CMP' is followed by a jump instruction. Use different jump instructions depending on the question requirements. Also, use register A_0 only to get an integer from the keyboard or to display its content on the screen. You might also find other restrictions in your actual test.

A brief illustration of these basic instruction rules is provided in the following examples.

Example 1

	MOV	A, 6	;A = 6
	ADD	A, 4	;A = 6 + 4 = 10
	INC	A	;A = A + 1 = 10 + 1 = 11
	DEC	A	;A = A − 1 = 11 − 1 = 10
	SUB	A, 6	;A = A − 6 = 10 − 6 = 4
	MOV	B, 8	;B = 8
	ADD	A, B	;A = A + B = 4 + 8 = 12
	SUB	A, B	;A = A − B = 12 − 8 = 4
JMP	Finish		;The program will jump to the label called Finish and leave the rest of program
End:	MOV	Result, 0	;Result = 0
	ADD	Result, A	;Result = Result + A = 0 + 12 = 12
	SUB	B, Result	;B = B − Result = 8 − 12 = −4
Finish:	ADD	A, B	;A = A + B = 4 + 8 = 12
	JMP	End	;The program will jump back to the label called End.

Example 2

Write a program using the basic commands shown in Table 3.1 to evaluate the arithmetical expression 10 + (12 − 4), first by using a single register (ie A); second by using two registers (ie A and B), leaving the results in register A.

First, using a single register:

MOV	A, 12	;A = 12
SUB	A, 4	;A = A − 4 = 12 − 4 = 8
ADD	A, 10	;A = A + 10 = 8 + 10 = 18

Second, using two registers:

MOV	A,12	;A = 12
MOV	B, 4	;B = 4
SUB	A, B	;A = A − B = 12 − 4 = 8
ADD	A, 10	;A = A + 10 = 8 + 10 = 18

You might sometimes be asked to start your program with 'BEGIN' and finish with 'END' or 'HLT' to terminate the program execution. Since we are using a hypothetical assembly language, this is considered to be a decorative rather than a necessary operation, and is not required in the following tests. But you may have to use it in your actual test.

Now imagine that you have been invited to sit an IT computer aptitude test. Read again the structure of the assembly language test carefully, understand fully the basic functions of the operation instructions in Table 3.1, and study the fundamental rules stated in 'Tips' for 30 minutes. Then try the following 14 questions and see how many programs you can write in 30 minutes.

1   Implement the following mathematical equations in assembly language using registers A and B:

$I = 1$

$I = I + 12$

$J = 6$

Then store the result $(I + J)$ in register A.

2   Implement the following expressions into assembly language using registers A, B and C:

$I = 10$

$I = I + 4$

$X = 9$

$Y = X - I$

3   Implement the following instructions in assembly language using registers A and B:

$X = 2$

If $X - Y = 0$ Then $X = X + 1$

Otherwise $Y = Y + 1$

4   Write a program that causes a jump to an instruction labelled ZERO if the value of the variable COUNT is zero, or to an instruction labelled EQUAL if the value of the variable COUNT is equal to 100. Otherwise to an instruction labelled OTHER using single register A.

5   Evaluate the following equation using two registers, A and B:

$(3 + 5)/(15 - 3)/(4/3) + (9/4) - (11/8) \times X = 0$

6   Write a program to evaluate the following expression using two registers, A and B:
$\{(11 - 2)/3(X + (6 \times 3/9) - I)\}$ Y

7   Compare two variables stored in registers A and B. If they are equal then add 20 to A and subtract 5 from B. If they are not equal then add 2 to A and subtract 2 from B.

8   Multiply two numbers, ie NUM1 and NUM2 by 4 and put the results in register A and B respectively.

9   Write a program to sum sequences 2, 4, 6, 8, 10 up to 30. Store the results in a variable called TOTAL-SUM, using registers A and B.

10 Write a program to sum the integers 1 to 30 by an increment of 1 every time and store the result in a variable called SUM, using registers A & B.

11 Write a program to add 15 consecutive numbers from 20 to 34 inclusive. Use registers A and B and accumulate the results in register C.

12 Write a program using the instruction 'GetInt' to input two integers X and Y from the keyboard to calculate $(X - Y)(X + Y)$. Then use the instruction 'ShoInt' to display the result on the screen using registers A, B, C and D.

13 Write a program to input two integers from the keyboard and display the smaller one. Use registers A and B.

14 Write a program where the positive integers are added to register A until a negative integer is input. Then display the sum of the numbers. Use registers A and B.

Spatial concepts

In this type of test you are often provided with the net of a benchmark unfolded box with a different pattern on each side. Your task is to build a three-dimensional image of the box. Then you have to compare the box from different angles and views with a set of boxes, and to decide which of these boxes matches the benchmark box, and mark your answer. Of course you have to twist and turn the box in different directions to be able to visualize the whole pattern. In this book I have presented you with four methods of visualization of the three-dimensional box by twisting and rotating the sides around the two identified bases, shown in Figures 3.3, 3.4, 3.5 and 3.6 and their solutions. The dotted line indicates the formation of the box around the two bases from two different angles sufficient to visualize the shape of the box. Study all the diagrams carefully and copy one or all the given diagrams and try to build a box and see how the patterns are arranged from different angles. Remember, a box always has six sides, no matter what.

Tips

- First identify the two bases (B) of the unfolded box and always use them as a benchmark to compare and view the other given boxes. Then follow one of the four methods presented in this book to build up the three-dimensional box. Twisting and rotating the sides by 90, 180 and 360 degrees towards the two identified bases will show you how the box will look if it is folded from different angles. In this way you will able to visualize how the pattern on each side is adjusted in relation to a different base from different angles.

- I recommend that in your test you spend a couple of seconds to draw a very quick and simple draft of what the shape of the folded box would look like from the view angle of the two bases before you start answering the questions. In doing this you will be assured that your answers will be correct; it will also save time and avoid unnecessary confusion.

- Different sizes and shapes of boxes may be used, ie rectangular for all sides or two sides wider than the other four sides, etc. The methods used in this book always hold; try to see for yourself. Again, identify the bases and then rotate the sides towards each base to form three-dimensional shapes from different angles.

FIGURE 3.3   Net

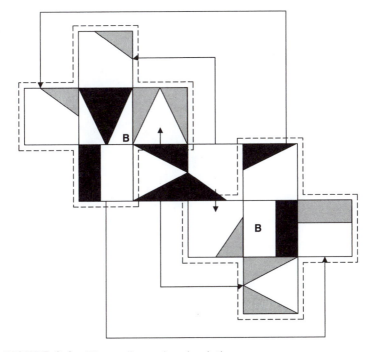

FIGURE 3.3   Three-dimensional solution

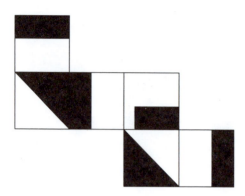

FIGURE 3.4   Net

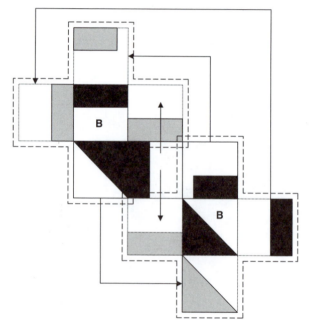

FIGURE 3.4   Three-dimensional solution

FIGURE 3.5   Net

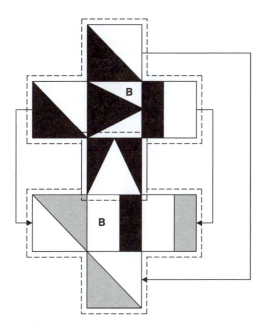

FIGURE 3.5   Three-dimensional solution

FIGURE 3.6   Net

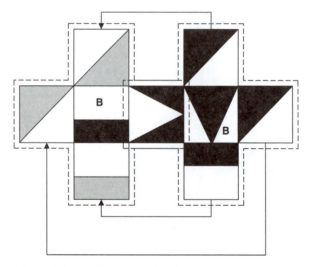

FIGURE 3.6   Three-dimensional solution

Now, look at Figure 3.7 and see how many of the associated questions in Figure 3.8 you can complete in three minutes. Compare your results with the answer given at the end of this chapter. To help you with this exercise I have provided the three-dimensional solution.

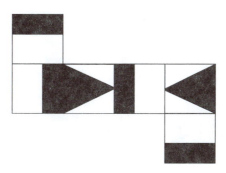

FIGURE 3.7   Net

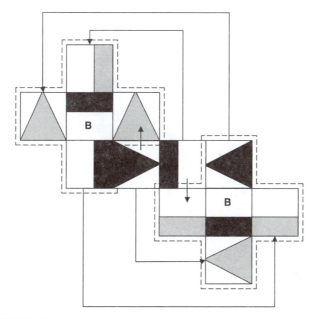

FIGURE 3.7   Three-dimensional solution

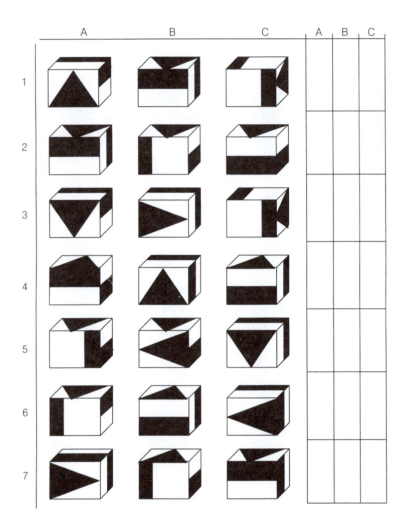

FIGURE 3.8

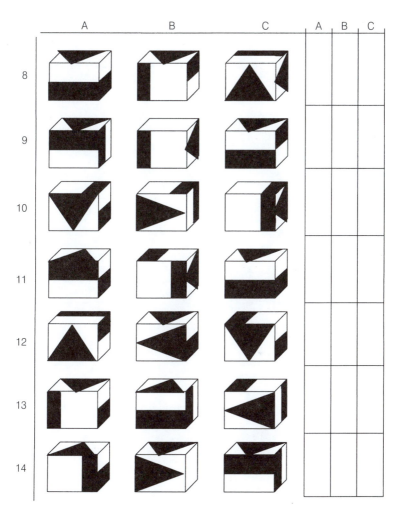

FIGURE 3.8   Con't

Answers for Chapter 3

Compiler checking by tracking error/line rules, and spatial concepts

	Compiler checking by tracking error		Compiler checking by line rules		Spatial concepts
1	SE	1	Z	1	A
2	NE	2	Y	2	C
3	OE	3	X, Y	3	B
4	SE, LE	4	X	4	C
5	SE	5	Y	5	C
6	OE	6	X, Y	6	B
7	LE	7	Z	7	C
8	SE	8	W	8	A
9	SE, OE	9	W	9	A
10	SE, OE	10	W, Y	10	C
11	SE, OE	11	X, Y	11	C
12	NE	12	Y	12	A
13	SE	13	Z	13	C
14	NE	14	X, Y	14	C
15	SE, LE	15	Z		
16	NE	16	W		
17	SE	17	Z		
18	LE	18	Z		
19	SE, LE	19	X, Y		
20	SE, OE	20	W, Y		
21	SE, LE, OE	21	W, X		
22	SE, LE	22	W		
23	OE	23	Y		
24	SE, OE	24	Z		
25	NE	25	W		

	Compiler checking by tracking error		Compiler checking by line rules		
26	SE, LE	26	Z		
27	SE, LE, OE	27	W, X		
28	OE	28	W, X, Y		
29	LE	29	W		
30	SE, LE	30	Z		
31	NE	31	Z		
32	NE	32	W		
33	OE	33	W		
34	SE	34	W		
35	SE, OE	35	Z		
36	SE, OE	36	W		
37	NE	37	X, Y		
38	LE	38	X		
39	NE	39	W		
40	NE	40	Y		
41	LE, OE				

Solutions for assembly language test

1
	MOV	A, I	;A = 1
	ADD	A, 12	;A = A + 12 = I + 12 = 1 + 12 = 13
	MOV	B, J	;B = J = 6
	ADD	A, B	;A = A + B = 13 + 6 = 19

2
	MOV	A, I	;A = I = 10
	ADD	A, 4	;A = A + 4 = 10 + 4 = 14
	MOV	B, X	;B = X = 9
	SUB	B, A	;B = B − A = X − A = 9 − 14 = −5

	MOV	C, Y	;C = Y
	MOV	C, B	;C = Y = B =
			X – A = –5

3

	MOV	A, X	;A = X = 2
	MOV	B, Y	;B = Y
	SUB	A, B	;A = A – B = X – Y
			= 2 – Y
	JMPZ	Next	;If X – Y = 0 then jump
			to label Next
	INC	B	;Otherwise, if X – Y ≠ 0
			then Y = Y + 1
Next:	INC	A	;X = X + 1

4

	MOV	A, COUNT	;A = COUNT
	JMPZ	ZERO	;If COUNT = 0,
			go to ZERO
	CMP	100	;Compare COUNT with 100
	JMPE	EQUAL	;If COUNT = 100 then
			go to EQUAL
	JMP	OTHER	;Otherwise go to OTHER

ZERO:
EQUAL:
OTHER:

5   After simplifying algebraic expressions you get: 22 – 11X = 0

	MOV	A, 11	;A = 11
	MUL	A, X	;A = 11X
	MOV	B, 22	;B = 22
	SUB	B, A	;B = B – A = 22 – 11X
	MOV	B, 0	;B = 0 = 22 – 11X

6   After simplifying algebraic expressions you get:
{3X + (2 – I)}Y

	MOV	A, 2	;A = 2
	SUB	A, I	;A = 2 – I
	MOV	B, 3	;B = 3

		MUL	B, X	;B = 3X
		ADD	B, A	;B = B + A = 3X + (2 – I)
		MUL	B, Y	;B = {3X + (2 – I)}Y

7		CMP	A, B	;Compare the content of registers A&B
		JMPE	Both-Equal	;If A = B then go to Both-Equal; Otherwise
		ADD	A, 2	;A = A + 2
		SUB	B, 2	;B = B – 2
	Both-Equal:	ADD	A, 20	;A = A + 20
		SUB	B, 5	;B = B + 5

8		MOV	A, NUM1	;A = NUM1
		ADD	A, A	;A = A + A = 2A
		ADD	A, A	;A = 2A + 2A = 4A
		MOV	B, NUM2	;B = NUM2
		ADD	B, B	;B = 2B
		ADD	B, B	;B = 4B

9		MOV	A, TOTAL-SUM	;A = TOTAL-SUM
		MUL	A, 0	;A = TOTAL-SUM = 0
		MOV	B, 2	;Set the counter using register B = 2
	Repeat:	CMP	B, 30	;If B = 30, then
		JMPE	Finish	;Go to label Finish ;Otherwise
		ADD	A, B	;TOTAL-SUM = A = A + B = 0 + 2 = 2
		ADD	B, 2	;B = B + 2 = 2 + 2 = 4
		JMP	Repeat	;Continue adding until you reach 30
	Finish:			

10		MOV	A, SUM	;A = SUM
		MOV	A, 0	;A = 0

	MOV	B, 1	;Set the counter B = 1
Repeat:	CMP	B, 30	
	JMPE	Finish	;If B = 30 go to Label Finish; Otherwise
	ADD	A, B	;A = SUM = SUM + B = 0 + 1
	INC	B	;B = B + 1 = 1 + 1 = 2
	JMP	Repeat	;Continue adding 1 to 30
Finish:			

11

	MOV	A, 15	;Initiate a counter
Begin:	MOV	B, 20	;Start value, B = 20
	MOV	C, 0	;C = 0
Repeat:	ADD	C, B	;C = C + B = 0 + 20
	INC	B	;B = B + 1 = 20 + 1 = 21
	SUB	A, 1	;A = A − 1 = 15 − 1 = 14
	JGO	Repeat	;Go to Repeat if A > 1

12

	GetInt		;Get an Integer from the keyboard and store A_0
	MOV	A, A_0	;Store the first value = X in register A
	GetInt		;Get the second Integer from the keyboard
	MOV	B, A_0	;Store the second value = Y in register B
	MOV	C, A	;C = X
	ADD	C, B	;C = C + B = X + Y
	MOV	D, A	;D = A = X
	SUB	D, B	;D = D − B = X − Y
	MUL	C, D	;C = C × D = (X + Y)(X − Y)
	MOV	A_0, C	;Transfer the content of register C to A_0
	ShoInt		;This command will display the content of A_0

13		GetInt		;Get first integer and store it in register A_0
		MOV	A, A_0	;Store the first integer in register A
		GetInt		;Get the second integer and store it in A_0
		MOV	B, A_0	;Store the second integer in register B
		CMP	B, A	;Compare the first and second integers
		JLO	Loop1	;Jump if the integer in register A $<$ B
		ShoInt		;Display the second integer
		JMP	Loop2	;Unconditional jump to Loop2 if needed
	Loop1:	MOV	A_0, A	;Otherwise transfer the first integer into A_0
		ShoInt		;Display the first integer
	Loop2:			

14		MOV	A, 0	;Clear register A = 0
	Loop1:	GetInt		;Get an integer from keyboard and store in A_0
		MOV	B, A_0	;Transfer the input integer to register B
		JNE	Loop2	;Jump to Loop2 if the input integer is negative
		ADD	A, B	;A = A + B
		JMP	Loop1	;Unconditional jump to Loop1
	Loop2:	MOV	A_0, B	;Transfer the content of B ready for display
		ShoInt		;Display the content of A_0

Chapter 4
Common verbal reasoning tests

There are a variety of verbal reasoning tests, such as missing words, word swapping, hidden sentences, spelling, sentence completion, sentence correction, grammatical, sentence sequence, analytical writing, data sufficient, rearranging letters in the right order, identifying words having the same or opposite meaning, verbal critical reasoning tests (VCR) and others. All of them specialize in testing certain uses of the English language. However, after contacting various organizations big and small, and many graduates and professionals who applied for jobs in management, finance and IT, I found VCR is the most popular and widely used, especially for management and finance recruitment, where reading documents or producing concise and meaningful materials, or writing reports and letters play a major part in the job requirement. For IT recruitment it depends on the positions the company are recruiting for. Take for example programming positions – the tests provided in Chapter 3 in this book are mainly used. However, assessment for other IT positions may include verbal reasoning tests as well as other tests from this book. In this chapter I have focused on VCR and rearranging letters in the right order tests.

Verbal critical reasoning (VCR) tests

The principal objective of the verbal reasoning tests is to test skills in understanding, evaluating and analysing arguments in written verbally complex passages and drawing logical conclusions between what the writer is implying in the claim and what is actually stated. The passages are followed by a number of statements and your task is to decide whether each statement is 'true' or 'false' (from the information given in the passage) or 'can't tell' (because further information is needed to support the claim). Ambiguity occurs when the meanings of words, phrases or statement are easily confused with actual assumptions in the passage. To make the test more difficult the subject of the passage and statements is usually a hot topic in the public domain, on which you may have prior knowledge and formed a particular opinion. VCR tests a comprehensive understanding of the English language (which is beyond the scope of this book) and most of the skills mentioned above are needed indirectly to be able to analyse the information logically and answer the questions correctly.

Tips

- Reading various papers, books, technical manuals and magazines would be a good start. However, you also need to develop your vocabulary, including synonyms and antonyms using a thesaurus or any other resource. You should also be able to question the facts: What is the writer's purpose or intent in making this claim? Is there a hidden message between the lines? Does the relationship between words or sentences make sense?

- You need to familiarize yourself with jargon words in your subject speciality, because often the assumptions on which the argument is built are concealed in the meaning of words.

- Always look at cue words in the passages such as 'if', 'since', 'because' and so on, which usually identify the reason or premises in support of the writer's claim.

- Never, ever, in your tests draw any conclusion based on your prior knowledge of the subject in the passage. Always confine yourself to the information given in the passage.

- Don't forget that all the information you need to make a decision is in the passage alone and that there is only one solution.

- Be careful when you see absolute words such as 'ever', 'all', 'always', 'definitely' and so on in the statement. Most of the time the answer is 'false' or 'can't tell'.

- Look out for words that are similar in meaning such as: 'propound' and 'proposed'; 'revamp' and 'renovate'; 'undignified' and 'unceremonious'; 'least profitable' and 'modest profit'; 'paradoxically' and 'in contrast'; and so on. They might appear sequentially in the passage and statement to confuse you.

- Be aware of words that sound alike such as: 'sight' and 'site'; 'horde' and 'hoard'; 'in' and 'inn'; 'precede' and 'proceed'; and so on. Make sure you understand their different meanings.

In this test, you are given eight passages. For each passage you are provided with a number of statements. Your task is to read each passage carefully and analyse and evaluate the given information logically, then choose one answer according to these rules:

- if the statement is True, write capital T;

- if the statement is False, write capital F;

- if you can't tell whether the statement is true or false because there isn't sufficient information to support the claim, write capital C.

You have 15 minutes to complete the test; start when you are ready.

British scientists using wireless communication are working on the next generation of all-terrain robotic explorers for Mars that will be able to go to regions where satellite images suggest that water once flowed or might still remain underground. Water is considered essential for the evolution of life and some scientists believe they have evidence, from a Martian rock, that the planet once had life. The big difference between the new all-terrain robot and Pathfinder, which was sent earlier, is that it can move on sandy slopes with 50-degree slants, and even reconfigure parts of its body to maintain its balance as it rolls over rough terrain, using cameras, sensors and new control software.

1   The main difference between the new and old robot to explore Mars is its agility.

Answer

2   The new all-terrain robots are able to control themselves in a way that they will be able to access and fully traverse the water region.

Answer

3   The concept of life throughout the universe will be accepted if water is found on Mars.

Answer

The two-year study by the respected Swedish Radiation and Nuclear Safety Authority suggests a potential new risk to health from mobile phones, with the discovery that their radiation emissions can damage human cells. It found the critical factor determining the radiation emissions were the length between the earpiece and the mobile phone antenna. However, researchers said that the findings were not strong enough to cast serious doubt on the safety of mobile phones. Cells in culture often behave differently from those in living tissue, and the study offers no evidence of adverse effects.

4 If someone is worried about radiation levels one should adopt a precautionary approach and limit the length of time using the mobile phone.

Answer [ ]

5 The Swedish Radiation and Nuclear Safety Authority has proposed that mobile phones can be a risk to your health.

Answer [ ]

6 Blood vessel cells cultured in the laboratory usually behave abnormally when bombarded with emissions even when they are within safety guidelines for mobile phones.

Answer [ ]

7 Hands-free wiring reduces radiation.

Answer [ ]

8 Mobile users have an increased health risk.

Answer [ ]

A confessed student cheater says academic pressure has made cheating a way to survive in universities. The better grades you have, the better job you get, the better you're going to do in life. And if you learn to cut corners to do that, you're going to be saving yourself time and energy. The Education Authority lamented the changes in universities' culture where grades and tests scores are more important than integrity. It seems honour is a concept of the past.

9 The Educational Authority welcomed the changes in universities' culture.

Answer [ ]

10 Students sometimes cheat due to academic pressure.

Answer [ ]

11 In the real world cheating is going to be acceptable, because it's how well you do that matters, not how morally you do it.

Answer [ ]

12 Honour is a concept of the past and students should do anything in order to succeed.

Answer [   ]

13 Only grades and scores decide one's future job prospects.

Answer [   ]

Most modern computers are designed using the 'Von Neumann' architecture and built using silicon transistor technology. The size of transistor on silicon chips has continued to decrease dramatically. But we're approaching the limits, because this will make the design expensive and also affect the packing density, speed of performance and hence the functionality, since increasing miniaturization reduces capacitance and interconnection length. As a result, it may be that progress with silicon technology ceases on economic grounds before the absolute physical limit is reached. In any case, the challenge is to find alternative technologies, which it is highly possible will be based on quantum-mechanics to replace the new generation of microprocessor chips.

14 Only reduction in capacitance can be expected in miniaturization of silicon chips.

Answer [   ]

15 Computer chips designed using 'Von Neumann' architecture are more likely to be replaced by quantum-mechanics.

Answer [   ]

16 Silicon chips are widely used technology in all old-generation microprocessors.

Answer [   ]

17 In the future quantum-mechanics will definitely replace the current silicon technology.

Answer [   ]

The National Hurricane Centre monitors the ocean and determines a weather disturbance is a tropical storm when it has winds above

50 mph. A tropical storm is upgraded to a hurricane when its winds climb higher than 75 mph. A normal season averages 10 named storms in the Atlantic, but last year 15 named storms occurred. The strength of a tropical storm can depend on how tightly the storm clouds are formed in the centre.

18   The strength of a hurricane can depend on how tightly the rotation storm clouds are formed around the eye of the storm.

Answer [   ]

19   If the wind has a speed of above 80 km/h a disturbance is upgraded to a tropical storm.

Answer [   ]

20   No more than 10 named storms hit the Atlantic every year.

Answer [   ]

21   The general public are always warned when a hurricane is in the area.

Answer [   ]

One-fifth of EU countries' population is 65 or older. In roughly the last 30 years, the growth in dual-earner families has grown by 30 per cent. Single parent families have increased, too, in the same period of around 1968 to 2002. Most of these single-parent families are headed by women, but there's a high growth rate among men leading single-parent families as well.

22   Most of the single-parent families in the UK are headed by women.

Answer [   ]

23   About 80 per cent of the EU population is under 65 years old.

Answer [   ]

24   Single-parent families in the EU usually get government support.

Answer [   ]

25 In the last 30 years the number of married couples where both spouses work has dropped in the EU.

Answer [ ]

26 Married couples with families are more stressed because of their career.

Answer [ ]

The US Surgeon-General last December warned that more than 61 per cent of Americans are considered obese, and obesity accounts for 300,000 deaths a year – putting it in the same league as tobacco. Obesity-related costs have reached an estimated $113 billion annually. Treating related conditions such as diabetes and heart failure absorbs nearly 8 per cent of health spending. Suing food-makers would be tricky. Food, unlike cigarettes, is not inherently harmful or addictive. Proving in court the link between a plaintiff's heart disease and a particular food is a big challenge. The solution to the problem, says Betsy Jones, chief-executive of a big food company, is education, balance, variety and moderation (in eating) and people undertaking physical activity.

27 The public must be educated to control obesity.

Answer [ ]

28 No one can really be sure if he or she is ill because of obesity.

Answer [ ]

29 Cigarettes and food are major health hazards that cannot be traced to the act of any human or organization.

Answer [ ]

30 The US government earns millions of dollars from food tax and tens of thousands of civilians are employed in the food industry.

Answer [ ]

31 Winning litigation against the food industry wouldn't be as difficult as in the tobacco industry.

Answer

32 Food will always be the main contributor to obesity.

Answer

Owing to the downturn in the IT market the FTSE suffered a sharp downturn of 11 per cent on Tuesday after falling to 3,860.3, its lowest point since September 1996. A drop in the stock below 3,500 is highly possible, but not likely. On Monday, Europe's most valuable stock market index dropped 5.4 per cent, its biggest one-day percentage fall since a 5.7 per cent loss on 11 September 2001. The Bank of England expected the nation's economy to grow 2.5 per cent and unemployment to fall to 1.5 per cent this year. and between 1.5 and 1.3 per cent respectively in 2003.

33 With slow growth in the economy and high uncertainties, the Bank of England is likely to keep its target for a key short-term interest rate low until economic recovery seems more likely.

Answer

34 The UK economy will definitely grow by 2.5 per cent this year.

Answer

35 The downturn in the UK stock market is due to 11 September.

Answer

36 The Bank of England expected that unemployment would drop by 0.2 per cent in 2003 as compared with 2002.

Answer

Rearranging letters in the right order

In this test you need to rearrange the given letters to form an appropriate word. Then you need to mark or cross one letter to indicate its position, ie first, middle or last, as shown in the examples below. To avoid confusion, usually very common words are used, the letters can be rearranged to produce only one meaningful word and no two identical letters in a group are used.

Examples

Mark the first letter of the word:

0	1	2	3	4	5	6	7
1	L	C	A	E			

0	1	2	3	4	5	6	7
1	X						

LACE: The letter 'L' is to be marked, being the first letter of 'LACE'. You need to put a cross in column 1.

Mark the middle letter of the word:

0	1	2	3	4	5	6	7
1	S	K	I	Y	R		

0	1	2	3	4	5	6	7
1	X						

RISKY: The letter 'S' is to be marked, as it is the middle letter of 'RISKY'. You need to put a cross in column 1.

Mark the last letter of the word:

0	1	2	3	4	5	6	7
1	S	E	U	M	O		

0	1	2	3	4	5	6	7
1		X					

MOUSE: The letter 'E' is to be marked, being the last letter of 'MOUSE'. You need to put a cross in column 2.

You have 24 minutes to complete the three tests. Skip any combination of letters you find difficult to figure out.

Test 1

Rearrange the following letter groups to form the names of well-known countries around the world and then mark the first letter of the word.

0	1	2	3	4	5	6	7
1	B	H	A	I	N	A	R
2	M	U	I	G	E	L	B
3	N	I	A	P	S		
4	A	C	N	H	I		
5	U	S	P	R	Y	C	
6	E	C	N	A	R	F	
7	Y	N	A	M	G	R	E
8	E	E	E	G	R	C	
9	R	E	G	I	N		
10	D	N	A	L	E	R	I
11	L	E	A	I	R	S	
12	N	A	P	A	J		
13	N	A	J	R	D	O	
14	A	A	Z	M	I	B	
15	O	C	I	X	M	E	

0	1	2	3	4	5	6	7
1							
2							
3							
4							
5							
6							
7							
8							
9							
10							
11							
12							
13							
14							
15							

Test 2

Rearrange the following letter groups to form the names of well-known capitals around the world and then mark the middle letter of the word.

0	1	2	3	4	5	6	7
1	E	B	J	I	I	N	G
2	O	C	I	I	S	N	A
3	A	P	I	S	R		
4	A	H	D	A	G	A	B
5	A	R	O	I	C		
6	K	Y	O	O	T		
7	A	O	I	F	S		
8	K	O	K	N	A	B	G
9	K	R	A	D	A		
10	A	B	R	A	T		
11	A	K	U	L	B		
12	I	B	O	I	A	N	R

0	1	2	3	4	5	6	7
1							
2							
3							
4							
5							
6							
7							
8							
9							
10							
11							
12							

Test 3

Rearrange the following letter groups to form the names of well-known cities around the world and then mark the last letter of the word.

0	1	2	3	4	5	6	7
1	O	R	I	A	C		
2	U	L	O	E	S		
3	R	L	N	I	E	B	
4	O	R	M	E			
5	H	C	C	G	O	A	I
6	G	O	S	A	L	W	G
7	S	O	G	A	L		
8	U	D	B	N	I	L	
9	S	C	O	O	W	M	
10	F	I	A	O	S		
11	I	E	N	N	A	V	
12	S	T	O	I	R	B	L

0	1	2	3	4	5	6	7
1							
2							
3							
4							
5							
6							
7							
8							
9							
10							
11							
12							

Answers for Chapter 4

Verbal critical reasoning tests

1	T	**9**	F	**17**	C	**25**	F	**33**	C
2	T	**10**	T	**18**	T	**26**	C	**34**	F
3	C	**11**	C	**19**	T	**27**	T	**35**	C
4	C	**12**	F	**20**	F	**28**	T	**36**	T
5	F	**13**	F	**21**	C	**29**	F		
6	C	**14**	F	**22**	C	**30**	C		
7	C	**15**	F	**23**	T	**31**	F		
8	F	**16**	C	**24**	C	**32**	C		

Rearranging letters in the right order

Test 1 – answers

0	1	2	3	4	5	6	7		0	1	2	3	4	5	6	7
1	B	H	A	I	N	A	R	BAHRAIN	1	X						
2	M	U	I	G	E	L	B	BELGIUM	2							X
3	N	I	A	P	S			SPAIN	3				X			
4	A	C	N	H	I			CHINA	4	X						
5	U	S	P	R	Y	C		CYPRUS	5						X	
6	E	C	N	A	R	F		FRANCE	6						X	
7	Y	N	A	M	G	R	E	GERMANY	7					X		
8	E	E	E	G	R	C		GREECE	8				X			
9	R	E	G	I	N			NIGER	9					X		
10	D	N	A	L	E	R	I	IRELAND	10							X
11	L	E	A	I	R	S		ISRAEL	11				X			
12	N	A	P	A	J			JAPAN	12					X		
13	N	A	J	R	D	O		JORDAN	13			X				
14	A	A	Z	M	I	B		ZAMBIA	14			X				
15	O	C	I	X	M	E		MEXICO	15					X		

Test 2 – answers

	0	1	2	3	4	5	6	7	
1	E	B	J	I	I	N	G		BEIJING
2	O	C	I	I	S	N	A		NICOSIA
3	A	P	I	S	R				PARIS
4	A	H	D	A	G	A	B		BAGHDAD
5	A	R	O	I	C				CAIRO
6	K	Y	O	O	T				TOKYO
7	A	O	I	F	S				SOFIA
8	K	O	K	N	A	B	G		BANGKOK
9	K	R	A	D	A				DAKAR
10	A	B	R	A	T				RABAT
11	A	K	U	L	B				KABUL
12	I	B	O	I	A	N	R		NAIROBI

	0	1	2	3	4	5	6	7
1			X					
2	X							
3					X			
4		X						
5				X				
6	X							
8				X				
9								X
10	X							
11		X						
12					X			
13								X

Test 3 – answers

	0	1	2	3	4	5	6	7	
1	O	R	I	A	C				CAIRO
2	U	L	O	E	S				SEOUL
3	R	L	N	I	E	B			BERLIN
4	O	R	M	E					ROME
5	H	C	C	G	O	A	I		CHICAGO
6	G	O	S	A	L	W	G		GLASGOW
7	S	O	G	A	L				LAGOS
8	U	D	B	N	I	L			DUBLIN
9	S	C	O	O	W	M			MOSCOW
10	F	I	A	O	S				SOFIA
11	I	E	N	N	A	V			VIENNA
12	S	T	O	I	R	B	L		BRISTOL

	0	1	2	3	4	5	6	7
1	X							
2		X						
3			X					
4				X				
5					X			
6						X		
7	X							
8			X					
9					X			
10		X						
11				X				
12								X

Chapter 5
Common numerical psychometric tests

All candidates applying for IT, finance and management jobs have to take a numerical test, to test their abilities to work with numbers. In this book I present three kinds of test that are widely used and which deal with basic principles of arithmetic (addition, subtraction, multiplication and division). Knowledge of mathematical terminology, symbols and processes such as percentage, ratio, roots, decimals, fractions, powers and exponents is usually required, so brush up your maths skills and consult your old maths book because the basics are not covered here. The first and second sections of this chapter deal with estimation, calculation and problem solving worked out without the use of a calculator. However, in section 3, which deals with the data interpretation of tables and graphs, you are free to use one. I urge you throughout this chapter to look at the given answer choice before working on the problem, to give you an idea of what you should expect and to help you to exclude unreasonable alternatives.

Numerical estimation

In this test you are presented with a variety of questions to which you must estimate the answer. Quick mental arithmetic can be carried out with the help of some scrap paper. However, in a real test you would have no time, so try to practise and familiarize yourself with these types of problem. Always keep in mind that you are never asked to supply an exact answer for the question; you are only asked to estimate which of the given choices is closest.

Tips

To give you practice in avoiding common mistakes:

- If you have to multiply/divide and add/subtract do the multiplication/division first as in this example:

  $20 - 5 + 9 \times 5 \div 5 = 20 - 5 + 45 \div 5 = 20 - 5 + 9 = 24$

- If you have to divide and multiply by the same number, then don't bother; one cancels out the other, as here:

  $(10 \div 5) \times 5 = 10$ or $20 + 5 \times 15 \div 15 = 25$

- Use quick mental arithmetic, for example:

292 + 398 + 102 + 801		A	B	C	D
		1598	1593	1590	1597

The quick mental arithmetic: $300 + 400 + 100 + 800$ gives a result of 1,600; therefore all the suggested answers A, B, C, D appear possible at first. However, if you add the remaining unit numbers you get $-8 - 2 + 2 + 1 = -7$. So only B can be the right answer, since $1,600 - 7 = 1,593$.

- Allocate your time effectively and leave the difficult questions for later if you still have time left.

Another way to develop your quick mental arithmetic skills is the Master Maths game; shown in Figure 5.1. This game is very simple and easy to play. It consists of a novel construction, rules, arrangements and characteristics adequate to provide numerical training for anyone wanting to improve their maths skills. It stimulates learning in dealing with numbers. I believe that by continuously playing the game, the basic mathematical principles will be embedded in your brain to be used in your daily life or in passing your psychometric tests.

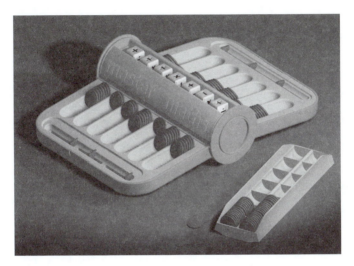

FIGURE 5.1

Now try the following test, which consists of 30 questions that must be answered within a time limit of 7 minutes. The questions range from very easy to quite challenging.

TABLE 5.1   Numerical estimation test

		A	B	C	D
1	$304 \div 2 + 15 - 25 = ?$	138	142	135	145
2	$4 + 6 \times 2 \div 2 \times 1 + 3 - 5 = ?$	8	6	5	10
3	$9\,^1/_4 + 10\,^3/_4 - 2\,^3/_2 + 2.5 = ?$	18	17	19	21
4	$6\,^2/_4 \div\,^1/_2 \times\,^4/_2 = ?$	7.5	7	6	6.5
5	$^{16}/_4 \times\,^{60}/_5 \div\,^{12}/_4 \times\,^{48}/_{12}$ $+\,^4/_{10} \times\,^{20}/_4 - 3 = ?$	4	3	5	6
6	$^1/_2 +\,^2/_6 +\,^7/_4 +\,^9/_2 -\,^8/_2 = ?$	6	4	3	5
7	$7 + 6.241 + 18.021 + 2.2 = ?$	29	30	35	33
8	$8.1 + 2.33 + 9.001 + 16.02 = ?$	35	37	33	31
9	$5.020 - 1.112 - 1.021 - 0.38 = ?$	2.8	2.5	2.9	2.7
10	$(7.5 + 55) / (0.05) + 10 = ?$	1270	1255	1260	1250
11	$(82 - 0.44) / (2.002) + 15 = ?$	54	56	58	59
12	$20\% + 15\% + 65\% + 1 = ?$	2	1	3	1.5
13	$13\% \times\,^2/_{65} + 10 = ?$	9.5	10.5	11	10
14	$50\% \times\,^{120}/_{50} +\,^{300}/_{100} + 100\%$ $- 2 = ?$	3.8	3	4	4.5
15	$7 + 58 + (-4) + 8 - (-5) = ?$	74	73	75	72
16	$-2 + (-6.2) - (-0.2) - (-5) = ?$	+3	−4	+4	−3
17	$-5.8 + 3 + (-2.18) - (-10.06)$ $+ (-1.08) = ?$	−4	4	3.5	−3.5
18	$-10 + 19 - (-2) + (-3) + (+2)$ $= ?$	10.5	9	10	11
19	$(-3)(+2) + (-10)(-2) -$ $(+2)(+4) = ?$	6	−2	5	−3
20	$(-9)(-2) + (-8)(-6) - (-5)(-4) = ?$	−46	46	−12	40

		A	**B**	**C**	**D**
21	$5426 - 3202 + 236 - 980 = ?$	-1480	1485	1475	1480
22	$9302 + 2105 - 9003 + 12 = ?$	2419	-2420	2416	2418
23	$120\,^1/_2 + 180\,^3/_4 - 50\,^1/_5 - 2\,^4/_5 = ?$	248	245	249	250
24	$12\,^2/_5 - 19\,^3/_4 + 6\,^6/_5 + 3\,^3/_2 = ?$	$4\,^7/_{25}$	$4\,^9/_{20}$	$4\,^5/_{18}$	$4\,^7/_{20}$
25	$-23 + 73\,^9/_6 + 19 - 22\,^5/_4 = ?$	49	$47\,^9/_6$	$46\,^5/_4$	52
26	$\sqrt{25} + \sqrt{36} - \sqrt{144} = ?$	13	$+1$	-1	0
27	$3\,\sqrt{25} + 3\,\sqrt{9} - 5\,\sqrt{49} = ?$	-11	10	-35	15
28	$2\,\sqrt{36} - 10\,\sqrt{9} + 3\,\sqrt{25} - 2\,\sqrt{49} = ?$	17	-17	15	-15
29	$8^{1/3} + 25^{1/2} + 9^{1/2} - 2 = ?$	10	9	7	8
30	$27^{1/3} + 125^{1/3} - 512^{1/3} = ?$	3	0	-1	1

Problem solving

This test requires, as well as knowledge of mathematical principles, an understanding of the fundamentals of algebra and arithmetic.

Tip

As they say, understanding the question is half the answer. Read carefully and make sure you know what is required of you. Avoid making assumptions about costs rising, etc. Use only the information given in the question. Try quick mental arithmetic if possible. Also, before you start this test, practise the mathematical operations presented in the previous section, as well as others such as averages, fractions, etc, which are useful for this section. Nearly all of the questions are easily answered once you have figured out how the question works. Don't perform unnecessary calculations if you can use quick mental arithmetic. The time you save can be used to check other questions.

The following test will give you the necessary confidence for the real test and help you to avoid unnecessary mistakes. Now try the test, which consists of 30 questions that must be answered within a time limit of 45 minutes.

1   How much will it cost to build a wooden fence round a house that is 25 metres wide and 75 metres long, if the cost of 50 cm is £10?

A	B	C
£4,000	£40,000	£400

Answer [   ]

2   It costs a publisher n pounds for each book to publish the first 1,000 books; extra books cost $n/6$ pounds each. How many pounds will it cost to publish 7,000 books?

A	B	C
7,000n	2,000n	5,000n

Answer [   ]

3   The distance between London and Hull is 300 miles. An Intercity train travels at 120 miles per hour from London to Hull. The train then goes back to London. If the total journey time was 4 hours and 30 minutes, what was the average speed of the Intercity train on the way back to London?

A   B   C
160 mph   140 mph   150 mph

Answer

4   At weekends the local Bowling club charges each person a flat rate of *n* pounds for up to four hours and $1/9n$ for each hour or fraction of an hour after the first three hours. How much does it cost for two people to go for six hours and 25 minutes at the weekend?

A   B   C
$6/9n$ $26/9n$ $13/9n$

Answer

5   John bought £3,000 worth of stocks in company X. He sold two-thirds of his stock after the value doubled, then sold the remaining stock at four times its purchase price. What was the total profit on the stock of company X?

A   B   C
£3,000   £4,000   £5,000

Answer

6   The price of a barrel of oil in 1998, 1999 and 2000 rose 10 per cent more over the previous year's price. How much more did the consumer have to pay in 2000 than in 1998?

A   B   C
19%   21%   23%

Answer

7 Assume British Airways owns 40 per cent of the stock in Virgin Atlantic Company. Easyjet owns 20,000 shares in Virgin. Midland owns all the shares not owned by British Airways or Easyjet. How many shares does British Airways own if Midland has 25 per cent more shares than British Airways?

A	B	C
80,000	75,000	100,000

Answer [   ]

8 Some market research in England of n young people under 15 years of age found that 30 per cent liked McDonalds. An additional x young people were asked and all of them liked McDonalds. Eighty per cent of all the young people in the market research claimed they liked McDonalds. Find n young people in terms of x.

A	B	C
3.5	2.5n	3

Answer [   ]

9 Peter, David and Tina ate lunch together. Tina's bill was 70 per cent more than David's bill. Peter's bill was 11/9 as much as Tina's bill. If David paid £10 for his lunch, approximately how much was the total bill that the three paid?

A	B	C
£48	£52	£45

Answer [   ]

10 A surveyor assessed the value of a house in the North of England at £85,000. The assessed value represented only 50 per cent of the market value of the house. If the HMRC taxes are £5 for every £1,000 of the market value of the house, how much are the total taxes on the house?

A	B	C
£800	£637.5	£850

Answer [   ]

11 A ton of potatoes costs £20, a ton of onions costs £29. If the price of potatoes rises by 15 per cent a month and the price of onions remains unchanged, how many months will it take before a ton of onions costs less than a ton of potatoes?

A	B	C
4	2	3

Answer [   ]

12 At one of the Save the Children's charity banquets for wealthy people, 30 per cent of the guests contributed £60 each, 55 per cent contributed £15 each and the rest contributed £5 each. Approximately what percentage of the total banquet takings came from people who gave £15?

A	B	C
31%	42%	26%

Answer [   ]

13 A microwave oven originally cost £200. Before Christmas it was on sale at 110 per cent of its original cost. After the New Year when the sale season started, the oven was discounted 15 per cent and was sold. The microwave oven was sold for what cost?

A	B	C
£253	£187	£220

Answer [   ]

14 There are 20 postmen in Crawley responsible for delivering mail. If a typical postman can deliver 30/2 mail in 30 minutes, how many pieces of mail should all postmen in Crawley be able to deliver in 3½ hours?

A	B	C
2,100	1,050	2,200

Answer [   ]

15   Butter costs half as much as cheese. Cheese costs 9/8 as much as milk. Milk costs what fraction of the cost of butter?

A	B	C
9/8	9/16	16/9

Answer [   ]

16   The total cost of typing a PhD thesis is £50. Merry typed 60 per cent of the thesis and Lina typed the rest. How much did Lina receive?

A	B	C
£20	£25	£30

Answer [   ]

17   On Monday a milkman delivered x bottles of milk, on Tuesday he delivered three times as many, and on Wednesday he delivered 120 bottles. Over the three days the milkman delivered 240 bottles. How many did he deliver on Tuesday?

A	B	C
30	90	120

Answer [   ]

18   An estate agent rented a house for £500 per month. Ten years later the tenant calculated that if he had bought the house and had a £200 per month mortgage he would have owned the house. How much would he have saved if he had bought the house?

A	B	C
£30,000	£24,000	£36,000

Answer [   ]

19 A team exploring the Amazon consists of 30 scientists. One third are women, two thirds are men. To obtain a team with 40 per cent women, how many men should be replaced by women?

A	B	C
2	5	8

Answer [   ]

20 An ice-cream machine produces 6,000 lollies per hour. Because of maintenance the machine is not operational for 22 minutes. How many lollies are not produced because of maintenance?

A	B	C
2,225	2,200	2,275

Answer [   ]

21 The following are car production figures for plant A in a week: on Monday 200 cars, on Tuesday 300 cars, on Wednesday 400 cars, on Thursday 650 cars, and on Friday 210 cars. What was the average car production for the week for plant A?

A	B	C
350	300	352

Answer [   ]

22 A corner shop in West London sells three newspapers, *The Guardian*, *The Times* and *The Independent*. The shop sells 90 copies of *The Guardian*, 80 copies of *The Times* and 60 copies of *The Independent*. Ten customers buy both *The Guardian* and *The Times*, 8 buy both *The Times* and *The Independent* and 14 buy both *The Guardian* and *The Independent*. Five customers buy all three papers. How many customers does the corner shop have?

A	B	C
188	98	158

Answer [   ]

23 A university flat consists of two bedrooms. Both rooms are square, and one room is 1 m larger in its length and width than the other. The university charges £2 per meter square per month. If a student pays £362 per month, what are the internal dimensions in metres for both rooms?

A	B	C
9×9 m and 10×10 m	11×11 m and 12×12 m	8×8 m and 9×9 m

Answer _____

24 Paul and his Dad, who live in a rural area of Bucks, decided to visit the shopping centre in Oxford Street in London. Paul cycled at an average speed of 25 km per hour and his Dad drove at an average speed of 55 km per hour. Paul left home first, and his Dad followed half an hour later. Approximately how far will Paul have travelled before his father catches up with him?

A	B	C
36 km	23 km	27 km

Answer _____

25 A farmer owns two fields, different in size, of 50 acres in total, in which he grows wheat. In 2007 he found that from the first field he reaped 100 kg of wheat per acre but from the second field only 80 kg per acre. At the end of the harvest season in 2007 he found that one field had produced 860 kg more than the other. What are the sizes of the two fields?

A	B	C
30 acres and 20 acres	15 acres and 35 acres	27 acres and 23 acres

Answer _____

26 Three overweight ladies, Nicki, Janet and Chris, in total weighed 850 kg. Nicki was the largest of the three, weighing twice as much as Janet, while Chris was only 50 kg heavier than Janet. What was the weight of the three overweight ladies?

A	B	C
200 kg, 400 kg, 250 kg	300 kg, 350 kg, 200 kg	200 kg, 300 kg, 350 kg

Answer [＿＿＿＿＿＿]

27 In Germany, Stephan earns €1,500 per month (gross). National Insurance (NI) contributions of 2 per cent, pension of 2 per cent and Income Tax (IT) of 35 per cent are then deducted and calculated on the gross earning. In Greece, using the same currency, the rates of NI, IT and pension are the same. However, in Greece the NI and pension are calculated on the net amount after deduction of IT. George, who lives in Greece, earns the same gross salary as Stephan. How much better off is George than Stephan?

A	B	C
€32	€21	€41

Answer [＿＿＿＿＿＿]

28 Geraldine has invested her yearly ISA allowance of £3,000 in a six-year bond in a bank's internet account. The account promises 6.50 per cent per annum and the bank will pay compound interest. How much will her investment be worth in six years?

A	B	C
£4,277.56	£4,110.25	£4,377.42

Answer [＿＿＿＿＿＿]

29   One day Dr Patel, a surgeon in Ealing Hospital, cycled from his home in West Drayton to Ealing, a round trip of 24 km. His average speed on the outward journey to Ealing was x km/h. Luckily, on his return home to West Drayton, there were no traffic jams and he managed to cycle 4 km/h faster and completed the return journey 16 minutes quicker than the outward journey to Ealing. Round all the numbers to one significant figure and calculate Dr Patel's average speed on the return journey to West Drayton.

A	B	C
19 km/h	21 km/h	23 km/h

Answer [   ]

30   Uxbridge College employs 400 teaching staff, of whom 70 per cent are women. The mean monthly salary of all teaching staff is £2,500. The mean monthly salary of the men is £2,400. What is the approximate mean monthly salary of the women?

A	B	C
£2,543	£2,434	£2,644

Answer [   ]

Interpretation of graphs and data

Being able to calculate and measure statistical information is very important for jobs in IT, finance and management.

Tips

- Scan the whole graph or table before you start answering the questions.

- Carefully read the units, ie cm, m, pounds, pennies, etc and make sure to answer in the correct unit.

- As before, read the choices before you answer, because many questions need a little calculation and more intelligent reading to understand them.

- A common mistake is mixing decimals and percentages, for example: 1/100 = 1% = 0.01; 10/100 = 10% = 0.1.

- Always use your common sense to see whether the answer makes sense.

Now work through the following examples and see how many you can finish in 60 minutes.

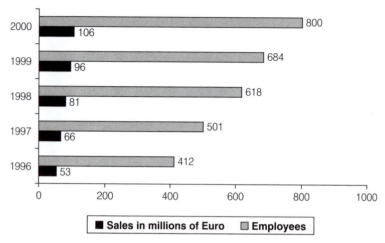

FIGURE 5.2 Continuous growth of sales and staff

1 By approximately what percentage did total staff numbers change from 1996 to 2000?

   A   B   C
   387   94%   90%

   Answer [   ]

2 By what percentage did the total profit change from 1996 to 2000?

   A   B   C
   100%   €53 million   50%

   Answer [   ]

3 If the number of employees in 2001 has increased by 25 per cent over 2000, what was the total number of new recruits in 2001 compared with 2000?

   A   B   C
   200   ˙1000   1200

   Answer [   ]

4   Between 1996 and 2000 which years showed the smallest and largest staff profit numbers?

A   B   C
1996 and 2000   1999 and 1996   1999 and 1998

Answer [   ]

5   If €1 = £ 0.65, then the profit in 1999 was approximately:

A   B   C
£6,240,000   £62.4 million   €624,000,000

Answer [   ]

6   If there are 300 additional recruits in 2001 and the average growth of sales and staff remains constant, how much greater would the total sales volume in euros for 2001 be?

A   B   C
£39.75 million   €3,975,000   €39,750,000

Answer [   ]

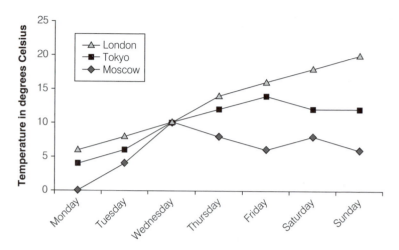

FIGURE 5.3 One week's temperatures in three capitals

1 On which day did the three capitals have the same temperature?

A	B	C
Monday	Wednesday	Friday

Answer [   ]

2 Which day showed the largest increase in temperature in Moscow?

A	B	C
Wednesday	Saturday	Monday

Answer [   ]

3 In which capital was the trend of temperature consistent throughout the week?

A	B	C
London	Moscow	Tokyo

Answer [   ]

4   What was the average temperature for the week in Moscow?

A	B	C
8°	4°	6°

Answer

5   What was the average temperature for the week in Tokyo?

A	B	C
7°	8°	10°

Answer

6   What was approximately the percentage increase in temperature between Monday and Sunday in London?

A	B	C
237	233%	245

Answer

7   What was the ratio of temperature in London on Sunday to the temperature in Moscow on Tuesday?

A	B	C
5:1	1:5	4/20

Answer

Total Income in 1990 £20000

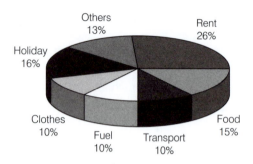

Total income in 2000 £35000

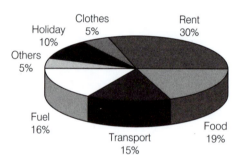

FIGURE 5.4 Income and expenditure for an average family between 1990 and 2000

1   The yearly expenditure on holidays in 1990 was 160 per cent of the amount spent on:

A	B	C
Transport in 1990	Food in 1990	Clothes in 2000

Answer [   ]

2   If the average family income in 2001 rises by 25 per cent over 2000 (and all expenditure percentages remain the same), how much will the average family spend on holidays in 2001?

A	B	C
£3,650	£3,500	£4,375

Answer [   ]

3 The combined expenditure in 1990 for transport, fuel and others was approximately the same as:

A Two-thirds the amount spent on rent in 1990

B The amount spent on food in 2000

C The amount spent on clothes and others in 2000

Answer ⬚

4 The combined average family expenditure in 2000 for fuel, food, clothes and holidays was what fraction of the annual income?

A   B   C

$^2/_3$ $^1/_2$ $^1/_4$

Answer ⬚

5 The amount spent on fuel in 2000 was the same as

A The amount spent on transport in 1990

B The amount spent on holidays in 1990

C The combined amount spent on food and others in 1990

Answer ⬚

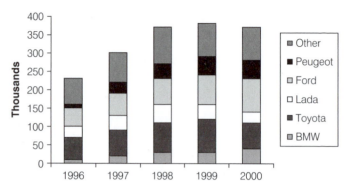

FIGURE 5.5   Number of cars sold in Europe

1   Approximately what percentage of cars sold in 2000 were Fords?

A	B	C
24%	30%	29%

Answer

2   From 1996 to 2000 of all the cars sold in Europe, the largest number of cars belonged to which manufacturer?

A	B	C
Ford	Peugeot	Toyota

Answer

3   Which car sales showed the most consistent increase between 1996 and 2000?

A	B	C
Lada	Ford	Peugeot

Answer

4   What was the average yearly number of cars sold by Toyota between 1996 and 2000?

A	B	C
74,000	7 million	820,000

Answer

5 Between 1996 and 2000, Peugeot car sales increased by what percentage?

A	B	C
50%	400%	40%

Answer

6 Which year showed the largest increase in other car sales over total car sales between 1996 and 2000?

A	B	C
2000	1999	1998

Answer

TABLE 5.2 Number of undergraduates, graduates and post-graduates of five universities between 1998 and 2000

University	1998 (in 000s)			1999 (in 000s)			2000 (in 000s)		
	U	G	P	U	G	P	U	G	P
AAA	10	2	2	12	2.5	1.5	13	3	1
BBB	15	3	4	14	3	3	12	2.5	2
CCC	20	5	4	22	5.2	4.1	23	5.5	4.2
DDD	18	2.5	2	19	3	1.5	21	3.1	1
EEE	22	4	1	23	4.1	0.5	25	4.2	0.5

Key: U: Undergraduates; G: Graduates; P: Postgraduates

1   Which university has shown a decline in undergraduate numbers every year over the period 1998–2000?

A	B	C
AAA	BBB	EEE

Answer [   ]

2   What was the percentage increase in the total undergraduate numbers in all five universities between 1998 and 2000 (to the nearest 4 per cent)?

A	B	C
7%	9	11%

Answer [   ]

3   Which universities had the same number of postgraduates and graduates between 1998 and 2000?

A	B	C
AAA and BBB	BBB and DDD	CCC and EEE

Answer [   ]

4   If in 2001 the number of undergraduate and postgraduate students in university EEE increased by 25 per cent and 200 per cent respectively over the year 2000, and the number of graduates remained the same, what approximately was the total number of undergraduates, postgraduates and graduates in university EEE in 2001?

A	B	C
369,500	0.3695 million	36,950

Answer

TABLE 5.3   Sales volume for five mobile phone companies over the last four years in thousands

Company	1996	1997	1998	1999	2000
Nokia	580	679	887	998	1187
Ericsson	294	493	548	598	632
Orange	192	232	268	312	366
Cellnet	120	209	204	302	366
BT	403	399	562	593	821

1   Which mobile phone companies have shown a decline in sales over the period 1996–2000?

A	B	C
Cellnet and BT	BT and Nokia	Ericsson and Cellnet

Answer [   ]

2   Of all these mobile phone companies (which showed a proportional increase in sales between 1999 and 2000), which showed the smallest and the largest increase as compared to 1999?

A	B	C
Cellnet and Ericsson	Ericsson and BT	BT and Orange

Answer [   ]

3   For all companies combined, what is the percentage increase in sales between 1998 and 1999 (to the nearest 4 per cent)?

A	B	C
11%	14%	12%

Answer [   ]

4   What are the average sales for Ericsson from 1996 to 2000?

A	B	C
0.05135 million	513,000	512,000

Answer

5   Which mobile company's sales volume in 2000 was approximately three times its sales in 1996?

A	B	C
Ericsson	Nokia	Cellnet

Answer

6   Which mobile company had the lowest increase in sales volume in 2000 compared to 1997?

A	B	C
Orange	Ericsson	Nokia

Answer

TABLE 5.4 EU members' statistical information in 2000

Country	Population in millions	Total employment in millions	% Below the poverty line	% Unemployed women in total unemployment	Total employment: unemployment
Portugal	10	5	29	49.5	2:1
Greece	12	6	24	57.5	5:2
UK	58	20	16	35.1	10:2
Spain	38	19	19	60.8	3:2
Italy	48	20	18	52.2	12:3
France	60	25	16	54.7	10:3
Netherlands	11	5.5	14	47.7	4:2
Belgium	13	5	13	30.5	8:3
Germany	68	34	13	58.5	9:3

1   Which country had the highest number of people below the poverty line in 2000?

   A   B   C
   France   UK   Spain

                                    Answer [   ]

2   What was the total number of unemployed men in Italy in 2000, in millions?

   A   B   C
   2.29   2.39   2.61

                                    Answer [   ]

3   The total number of unemployed women in 2000 was about x million in Belgium, with x equal to about:

   A   B   C
   2.43   0.57   1.3

                                    Answer [   ]

4   If in 2000 the unemployed women aged 60 or over made up only a third of the total unemployed women in Greece, how many men aged 60 or over were unemployed?

A   B   C
Can't say   1.38 million   0.46 million

Answer [   ]

5   The ratio of population in 2000 between France and Portugal was?

A   B   C
10/60   1:6   6:1

Answer [   ]

6   Which countries had the highest and lowest number of un-employed men in 2000?

A   B   C
Spain and   Germany and   Germany and
Greece   Portugal   Greece

Answer [   ]

In England, if you want to obtain a driving licence, first you should sit and pass your theoretical driving test. Then and only then can you apply to take a practical driving test. Table 5.5 shows the results from six practical driving test centres in England for all applicants, in hundreds, who passed and failed their driving test, assuming that the applicants took the theoretical and the practical test in the same year.

TABLE 5.5 The results of six driving test centres in England

	Driving Centre	Result	1998	1999	2000	2001	2002
1	London	Passed	112	69	62	86	119
		Failed	121	96	102	89	191
2	Manchester	Passed	100	89	94	54	66
		Failed	116	99	96	58	68
3	Warwick	Passed	54	69	96	86	109
		Failed	95	130	97	84	112
4	Oxford	Passed	22	66	23	99	101
		Failed	44	87	44	102	111
5	Swansea	Passed	53	56	61	80	45
		Failed	62	75	72	81	50
6	Hull	Passed	70	82	70	31	10
		Failed	75	86	73	81	20

1 What was the total number of applicants in hundreds who passed the theoretical driving tests in 2001 and 2002?

A   B   C
931   1,933   2,159

Answer [   ]

2 In which year did more applicants pass their practical driving test than failed in Warwick?

A   B   C
1999   2000   2001

Answer [   ]

3   Of the total number who obtained a driving licence in 2002, what percentage was from Swansea?

A   B   C
10%   12.5%   15%

Answer [   ]

4   In which driving centre has the number of failed practical driving tests declined every year over the period 1998–2001?

A   B   C
Hull   London   Manchester

Answer [   ]

5   What was the ratio of the number of applicants who obtained a driving licence in Manchester in 1998 to the number who failed the practical driving tests in Hull in 2002?

A   B   C
1:5   5:1   10:1

Answer [   ]

6   In which driving test centre did more applicants obtain a driving licence between 1998 and 2002?

A   B   C
Warwick   Can't say   London

Answer [   ]

TABLE 5.6 Percentage increase in average family monthly expenditure since 2002 in the UK

Product	Average family monthly expenditure in £	% increase on 2002 rate						
	2002	2003	2004	2005	2006	2007	2008
Rent	600.00	2.5	3.9	7.5	8.8	10.5	11.3
Bills	25.00	1.1	2.3	6.4	10.8	18.6	20.8
Petrol	30.00	2.3	4.6	6.8	11.8	19.5	22.3
Council Tax	70.00	2	2.5	3	3.5	4	4.5
Transport	20.00	2.2	5.2	7.6	9.2	14.8	18.6
Clothes	30.00	2.1	3.4	4.2	6.5	7.3	8.5
Food and Drink	130.00	1.3	2.5	4.5	5.8	7.9	10.5
Others	55.00	0.2	1.2	2.11	3.2	4.5	5.1
Total expenditure	960.00						

1   If the average UK family rented the same dwelling in 2008 as they did in 2002, approximately how much would their monthly rent bill be in 2008?

A	B	C
£668.00	£696.80	£868.00

Answer ☐

2   If the total monthly expenditure of the average UK family in 2002 increased by 45 per cent in 2008, approximately how much will the average UK family have left after paying rent, Council Tax and bills?

A	B	C
£692.50	£621.00	£799.50

Answer ☐

3   If Janet Stephen's family buy 17 per cent more clothing and 7 per cent less food and drink per month in 2002 than the average UK family, while their other expenditures are the same as the average, by approximately how much does their monthly expenditure differ from the UK average family monthly expenditure?

A	B	C
+£5.10	+£4.00	−£4.00

Answer [   ]

4   How much will the average UK family spend each month in 2008 on rent, bills, petrol, Council Tax, transport and clothes?

A	B	C
£864.11	£968.50	£766.18

Answer [   ]

5   Approximately what is the percentage increase in average family monthly expenditure in the UK in 2008 compared to 2002?

A	B	C
15%	11%	17%

Answer [   ]

Answers for Chapter 5

Numerical estimation and problem solving

	Numerical estimation		Problem solving
1	B	1	A
2	A	2	B
3	C	3	C
4	D	4	B
5	B	5	C
6	C	6	B
7	D	7	A
8	A	8	B
9	B	9	A
10	C	10	C
11	B	11	C
12	A	12	A
13	D	13	B
14	B	14	A
15	A	15	C
16	D	16	A
17	B	17	B
18	C	18	C
19	A	19	A
20	B	20	B
21	D	21	C
22	C	22	A
23	A	23	A
24	D	24	B
25	C	25	C

	Numerical estimation		Problem solving
26	C	26	A
27	A	27	B
28	B	28	C
29	D	29	B
30	B	30	A

Interpretation of graphs and data – answers

Figure 5.2

1	B	4	B
2	A	5	B
3	A	6	C

Figure 5.3

1	B	5	C
2	A	6	B
3	A	7	A
4	C		

Figure 5.4

1	A	4	B
2	C	5	C
3	B		

Figure 5.5

1	A	4	A
2	C	5	B
3	B	6	C

Table 5.2

1	B	3	A
2	C	4	C

Table 5.3

1	A		4	B
2	B		5	C
3	B		6	A

Table 5.4

1	A		4	A
2	B		5	C
3	B		6	A

Table 5.5

1	B		4	C
2	C		5	B
3	A		6	A

Table 5.6

1	A		4	A
2	B		5	B
3	C			

Tips on solving the problems in problem solving

1   The perimeter of the house is 2 × lengths + 2 × widths = 2l + 2w or 25 + 25 + 75 + 75 = 200. The total cost is £10 × 200/0.5 = £4,000, therefore A is correct.

2   The first 1,000 books cost n pounds for each book, so altogether they will cost 1000n. The total cost is 1000n + 6000 × n/6 = 2000n, therefore B is correct.

3   Distance = speed × time: 300 = 120 × time; time = 2.5 hours from London to Hull.

   Total journey took 4 hours and 30 minutes, so the time from Hull to London is 4.5 − 2.5 = 2 hours. The speed = 300/2 = 150 mph, therefore C is correct.

4   For one person, cost $= n + 1/9 \times 4n = 13/9n$. For two people, multiply by two, therefore B is correct.

5   John sold his stock at $2/3 \times £3,000 = £2,000$. The value was doubled $= 2 \times £2000 = £4000$; and he made a profit of £4,000 $- £2,000 = £2,000$.

 The remaining stocks £3,000 $-$ £2,000 $=$ £1,000 were sold at £1000 $\times$ 4 $=$ £4,000 and the profit he made was £4,000 $-$ £1,000 $=$ £3,000, so the total profit was £2,000 $+$ £3,000 $=$ £5,000, therefore C is the correct answer.

6   Let x denote the price in 1998. In 1999 the price rose to 110 per cent of x which is $(1.1)x$, and in 2000 the price rose to 110 per cent of $(1.1)x$, which is $(1.1)(1.1)x$ or $1.21x$. Therefore the price of oil rose by 21 per cent more in 2000.

7   If Midland owns 25 per cent more than British Airways and British Airways owns 40 per cent of Virgin Atlantic, then Midland must own $1.25 \times 0.4 = 50$ per cent of Virgin Atlantic, since Easyjet $= 100\% - 40\% - 50\% = 10\%$.

 If 10 per cent of the shares in Virgin Atlantic is 20,000 shares, then there must be 200,000 shares in Virgin Atlantic. British Airways shares are $= 200,000 \times 0.4 = 80,000$, so A is the correct answer.

8   The total number of people researched is $0.3n + x = 0.8(n + x)$. $x = 2.5n$, so B is the correct answer.

9   Cost of Tina's lunch $= 1.7$ David's, and Peter's $= 11/9$ Tina's, so Peter's $= 11/9 \times 1.7$ David's $= 2$ David's. David paid £10 for his lunch, therefore Peter paid £20 and Tina paid £17, and the total bill for the three of them was approximately £48.

10   First find the market value of the house, which means £85,000/.5 $=$ £170,000. The tax rate is £5 for every £1,000 or 0.005. Therefore the total tax is $0.005 \times £170,000 = £850$.

11   The price of potatoes will be £20 $(1.15)n$. After n months the price must be greater than £29. When $(1.15)n$ is greater than £29/£20 $=1.45$. Since $1.15 \times 1.15 = 1.32$ and $1.15 \times 1.15 \times 1.15 = 1.52$, after three months the cost of a ton of onions will be less than the cost of a ton of potatoes.

12   Assume 100 people were invited. Therefore 30 per cent represents 30 people, who contributed £60, and 55 per cent represents

55 people, who contributed £15, and the rest represents 15 per cent or 15 people, who contributed £5. The total amount of contribution is £2,700, and the percentage of the total banquet takings coming from people who gave £15 = 825/£2,700 = 31%, so answer A is correct.

13 Since 110% of £200 = £220, the microwave was offered before Christmas for sale at £220. It was sold for (100% − 15%) = 85% of £220, since there was a 15% discount. Therefore the microwave was sold for 0.85× £220 = £187.

14 Since 30 minutes is ½ of an hour, in 3.5 hours the postmen should deliver: 20 × 7 × 30/2 = 2,100 pieces of mail.

15 Butter = ½ cheese, and cheese = 9/8 milk. Therefore butter = ½ × 9/8 milk, and milk's cost as a fraction of butter is milk/butter = 16/9.

16 Merry typed 60% × £50 = £30, therefore Lina typed £20 worth of the PhD thesis.

17 Assume on Monday the milkman delivered x bottles of milk; on Tuesday he delivered $3x$ and on the Wednesday delivered 120. The total is $x + 3x + 120 = 240$, therefore $x = 30$, and on Tuesday he delivered $3x = 3 \times 30 = 90$ bottles of milk.

18 Rent on the house for 10 years is £500 × 10 × 12 = £60,000. If the tenant had bought the house, the mortgage would have been £200 × 10 × 12 = £24,000, so he would have saved £36,000.

19 We have 10 women and 20 men in the team. To obtain 40% women, we need 40% × 30 = 12. We already have 10, so we need another 2. The answer is A.

20 Number of lollies per minute = 6,000/60 = 100. We have 22 minutes × 100 = 2,200.

21 The average is (200 + 300 + 400 + 650 + 210)/5 = 352.

22 Five customers buy all three newspapers. Ten buy *The Guardian* and *The Times*, 8 buy *The Times* and *The Independent*, and 14 buy *The Guardian* and *The Independent*. Since 90 buy *The Guardian*, the number who buy *The Guardian* only must be 90 − 10 − 14 − 5 = 61. Eighty buy *The Times*, so the number who buy *The Times* only is 80 − 10 − 8 − 5 = 57. Sixty buy *The Independent*, so the number who buy *The Independent* only is

60 – 8 – 14 – 5 = 33. Thus the corner shop has 61 + 10 + 57 + 8 + 33 + 14 + 5 = 188 customers.

23 Let x m be the length and width of the first room and $x + 1$ m will be the length and width of the next room. Total rent = 362 = $2x^2 + 2(x + 1)^2$. If you substitute $x = 9$, the equation will be equal and is the right answer. Therefore the smallest room will measure 9 × 9 m and larger room 10 × 10 m.

24 Let x be the time elapsed. Time = Distance/Average Speed, 25(30 + x)/60 = 55 (x/60),
750 + 25x = 55x, x = 25 minutes. Distance before his father catches up with him = 25 (55/60) = 23 km.

25 This little problem is best solved by simple algebra. Divide the area of the field into two and let x = the difference between the two fields. The total difference between the amounts the two fields produce is 860 kg.
100 (25 + x) – 80 (25 – x) = 860, x = 2.
The first field = 25 + 2 = 27; the second field = 25 – 2 = 23.

26 Nicki = N, Janet = J and Chris = C. N + J + C = 850.
N = 2 J
C = J + 50
2J + J + J + 50 = 850
4J = 850 – 50 = 800, J = 200 kg, substitute above and you will get N = 400 kg, H = 250 kg.

27 Stephan's net monthly salary: NI + IT + Pension = 39% × 1,500 = 585; 1,500 – 585 = €915.
George: IT: 35% × 1,500 = 525; 1,500 – 525 = €975. Net monthly salary: 975 – 975 × 4/100 = €936. Therefore George is 936 – 915 = €21 better off than Stephan.

28 Compound interest means the internet bank will pay interest on the interest. The table on page 182 shows how much Geraldine's investment will grow over six years.

Year	Amount invested	Interest	Total amount
1	3000	3000 × 0.065 = 195	3000 + 195 = 3195
2	3195	3195 × 0.065 = 207.675	3195 + 207.675 = 3402.675
3	3402.675	3402.675 × 0.065 = 221.173	3402.675 + 221.173 = 3623.848
4	3623.848	3623.848 × 0.065 = 235.550	3623.848 + 235.550 = 3859.398
5	3859.398	3859.398 × 0.065 = 250.860	3859.398 + 250.860 = 4110.258
6	4110.258	4110.258 × 0.065 = 267.166	4110.258 + 267.166 = 4377.424

Or you could calculate the compound interest using the following equation:

Amount invested after n years = original amount x (increased interest)^n = 3000 × $(1.065)^6$; = 3000 × 1.4591 = £4,377.42.

29   Time = (distance)/(average speed)

Outward time = 24/X. Put average speed on the return journey = Y km/h, Y = X + 4.

Return journey time = 24/Y = 24/(X + 4).

24/X − 24/(X + 4) = 16 minutes = 16/60 = 4/15 hours.

24.15 (X + 4) − 24.15X = 4X(X + 4), 360X + 1440 − 360X = $4x^2$ + 16X

X + 4X − 360 = 0.

Solve the quadratic equation using the formula y = −b ± $\sqrt{b^2}$ − 4ac/2a

a = 1, b = 4, c = −360; y = −4 ± $\sqrt{1456}$/2 = −4 ± 38.15/2

The two solutions (roots) are y ≈ −21 and y ≈ 17. Speed cannot be negative, so y ≈ 17.

Dr Patel's average speed on the return journey is X + 4 = 17 + 4 = 21 km/h.

30   Number of women staff W = 70/100 × 400 = 280; number of men staff M = 120.

The mean monthly salary of the men + the mean monthly salary of the women/400 = 2,500

The mean monthly salary of the men = 2,400 × 120 = 288,000

The mean monthly salary of the women = 1,000,000 − 288,000 = 712,000/280 = 2,542.85 ≈ £2,543.

Tips on solving the problems in interpretation of graphs and data

Figure 5.2 Continuous growth of sales and staff

1   In 1996 the total staff number was 412 and in 2000 it was 800. Therefore the total staff increase expressed as a percentage between 1996 and 2000 is (800 − 412)/412 × 100 = 94.17% ≈ 94%.

2   The total profit changes expressed as a percentage between 1996 and 2000 is (106 − 53)/53 × 100 = 100%.

3   Number of employees in 2001 is 25% × 800 + 800 = 1,000, and the total number of new recruits in 2001 is 1000 − 800 = 200.

4   The staff profit ratio for:
1996: 412/53 = 7.77
1997: 501/66 = 7.59
1998: 618/81 = 7.62
1999: 684/96 = 7.125
2000: 800/106 = 7.54
Therefore in 1999 the staff profit ratio was the smallest, and in 1996 the largest.

5   If €1 is equivalent to £0.65, then profit in 1999 is 96 × 0.65 = £62.4 million.

6   Total number of employees in 2001: 800 + 300 = 1,100, since the average growth of sales and staff remain constant compared to 2000. Therefore the total sales is (106 × 1100)/800 = 145.75 and this amount was greater than in 2000 by 145.75 − 106 = €39.75 million = €39,750,000. Check the decimal number in multiple-choice questions carefully to ensure that the number is in millions of euros.

Figure 5.3 One week's temperatures in three capitals

1   The answer is B, since all three capitals have the same temperature on Wednesday.

2   The answer is A; the steepest gradient for the week's temperatures in Moscow occurred from Tuesday to Wednesday.

3   Scanning the graph it is clear that London shows a consistent increase of temperature from Monday to Sunday.

4   The average temperature for the week in Moscow is $(0° + 4° + 10° + 8° + 6° + 8° + 6°)/7 = 6°$.

5   The average temperature for the week in Tokyo is $(4° + 6° + 10° + 12° + 14° + 12° + 12°)/7 = 10°$.

6   The temperature in London on Monday was 6° and on Sunday 20°; the approximate percentage increase over the week is $20° - 6°/6° × 100 = 233.33\% ≈ 233\%$.

7   The temperature in London on Sunday was 20° and the temperature in Moscow on Tuesday was 4° and the ratio is $20°/4° = 5/1 = 5:1$.

Figure 5.4 Income and expenditure for an average family between 1990 and 2000

1   Here you will find the ratio of the percentages. In 1990, 16% of the expenditure was for holidays. We want x where 160% of $x = 16\%$, so $x = 10\%$. Any category that received 10% of 1990 expenditures gives the correct answer. By looking at the pie graph it is obvious that transport in 1990 is the correct answer.

2   The average family income in 2001: $25\% × 35,000 + 35,000 = £43,750$. If the percentage expenditure on holidays in 2001 is similar to 2000 and equals 10%, then the average family expenditure on holidays in 2001: $£43,750 × 10\% = £4,375$.

3   By adding the percentages for transport, fuel and others in 1990 we get $10\% + 10\% + 13\% = 33\%$, therefore the combined expenditure is $33\% × £20,000 = £6,600$. Now you have to compare this figure with the three relationships given as multiple choices in A: $3/2 × 26\% × £20,000 = £346.66$, which is not correct. Then B: $19\% × £35,000 = £6,650$. Finally C:

5% × £35,000 = £1,750 which is incorrect. Therefore B is the closest value and is the correct answer.

4 By adding all the expenditures – fuel, food, clothes and holidays – we get 16% + 19% + 5% + 10% = 50% = 1/2, therefore B is the correct answer.

5 The amount spent on fuel in 2000 is 16% × 35,000 = £5,600. Now evaluate the given three multiple choices to find any equivalent: A: 10% × 20,000 = £2,000; B: 16% × 20,000 = £3,200; C: 15% + 13% = 28% × 20,000 = £5,600, which is the correct answer.

Figure 5.5 Number of cars sold in Europe

To compare several categories by a graph of the cumulative type, where the bar is divided up proportionately among different quantities, needs careful evaluation of each quantity. To make the quantities clear to you and help you to understand the graph, I have prepared a simple table with all the quantities.

	BMW	Toyota	Lada	Ford	Peugeot	Other
1996	10	60	30	50	10	70
1997	20	70	40	60	30	80
1998	30	80	50	70	40	100
1999	30	90	40	80	50	90
2000	40	70	30	90	50	90

1 Total cars sold in 2000 in thousands were 40 + 70 + 30 + 90 + 50 + 90 = 370 and the percentage of Ford cars sold in 2000 is 90/370 × 100 = 24.32% ≈ 24%.

2 To find which manufacturer sold the most cars, calculate the numbers of cars sold in thousands between 1996 and 2000 for the three models given in your multiple choices:
Ford: 50 + 60 + 70 + 80 + 90 = 350
Peugeot: 10 + 30 + 40 + 50 + 50 = 180
Toyota: 60 + 70 + 80 + 90 + 70 = 370
Therefore Toyota sold the highest number of cars in thousands between 1996 and 2000.

3   By scanning all the quantities in the table above, it is clear that Ford had consistently increased its car sales between 1996 and 2000.

4   The average number of cars sold by Toyota between 1996 and 2000 in thousands: (60 + 70 + 80 + 90 + 70)/5 = 74. Make sure you know where the decimal point is and that the number is multiplied by thousands.

5   Peugeot car sales expressed as a percentage between 1996 and 2000 in thousands: (50 − 10)/10 × 100 = 400%.

6   Scanning the table above you find that in 1998 'other' car sales were the largest between 1996 and 2000.

Table 5.2 Number of undergraduates, postgraduates and graduates of five universities between 1998 and 2000

1   Simply scanning the table may be the best strategy here, all you need to do is find one of the three universities given in the multiple choices where the number of undergraduates declined between 1998 and 2000. Here University BBB shows a decline in undergraduate numbers every year over the period 1998–2000, and is the correct answer.

2   Important note. Carefully add all the figures in questions like this, otherwise the round number may be calculated differently and that may lead you to choose the wrong answer in multiple choices, which are deliberately designed with the options very near to each other.

Total undergraduate numbers in thousands in all five universities in 1998 was 10 + 15 + 20 + 18 + 22 = 85.

Total undergraduates numbers in thousands in all five universities in 2000 was 13 + 12 + 23 + 21 + 25 = 94.

The increase expressed as a percentage: (94 − 85)/85 ×100 = 10.58% = 11%.

3   Scanning the table carefully for all five universities you will find that university AAA has 2,000 postgraduates and graduates in 1998 and university BBB has 3,000 postgraduates and graduates in 1999. No other university shows similar characteristics. Therefore AAA and BBB is the correct answer.

4   In 2001 the number of undergraduates in thousands in university EEE: 25% × 25 + 25 = 31,250. The number of postgraduates in 2001 is 200% × 0.5 + 0.5 = 1,500 respectively. However, the number of graduates remains the same for 2001; the total number is 4,200 + 31,250 + 1,500 = 36,950. Again check your decimal point carefully.

Table 5.3 Sales volume for five mobile phone companies over the last four years in thousands

1   By scanning the table for all five mobile companies, you will find that Cellnet and BT have shown a decline in sales over the period 1996–2000.

2   All five mobile companies showed an increase in sales between 1999 and 2000.
Nokia's increase was: 1,187 – 998 = 189, so the proportional increase was 189/998 = 0.189.
Ericsson's increase was: 632 – 598 = 34, so the proportional increase was 34/598 = 0.056.
Orange's increase was: 366 – 312 = 54, so the proportional increase was 54/312 = 0.173.
Cellnet's increase was: 366 – 302 = 64, so the proportional increase was 64/302 = 0.211.
BT's increase was: 821 – 593 = 228, so the proportional increase was 228/593 = 0.384.
Therefore the smallest proportional increase is 0.056 (for Ericsson) and the largest proportional increase is 0.384 (for BT).

3   The total sales in thousands for all mobile companies
in 1998: 887 + 548 + 268 + 204 + 562 = 2469;
in 1999: 998 + 598 + 312 + 302 + 593 = 2803
The increase expressed as a percentage: (2,803 – 2,469)/2469 × 100 = 13.52% and to the nearest 4% is 14%.

4   The average sales for Ericsson in thousands between 1996 and 2000 is (294 + 493 + 548 + 598 + 632)/5 = 513,000.

5   Scan the table for all five mobile companies and you will find that Cellnet sales were 366,000 in 2000, compared to 120,000 in 1996, which is approximately three times and is the correct answer.

6   Scan the table for the three multiple choices – Orange, Ericsson, Nokia – and don't waste time calculating others not included. The lowest increase in sales in thousands for Orange between 1997 and 2000 was 366 – 232 = 134, for Ericsson 632 – 493 = 139 and for Nokia 1,187 – 679 = 508. Therefore Orange has the lowest increase in sales volume in 2000 as compared with 1997.

Table 5.4 EU members' statistical information in 2000

1   Again, only perform the calculation for the three countries given in your multiple choices and don't waste time.
    Number of people in millions below the poverty line in France: 16% × 60 = 9.6; in the UK: 16% × 58 = 9.28; in Spain: 19% × 38 = 7.22. Therefore France has the highest number and A is correct.

2   Let x be the total unemployment (men and women), then for Italy total employment/total unemployment in millions: 12/3 = 20/x. x = 5 million unemployed (men and women), from which 52.2% × 5 = 2.61 million are unemployed women and 5 – 2.61 = 2.39 million are unemployed men.

3   Let x be the total unemployment (men and women), then for Belgium total employment/total unemployment in millions in Belgium: 8/3 = 5/x. x = 1.875 million unemployed (men and women), from which 1.875 × 30.5% = 0.57 million are unemployed women.

4   We cannot say, because there is no information in the table that shows any details of unemployed men or women aged 60 or over. The table has only general unemployment figures; therefore, we cannot answer the question.

5   The ratio of population between France and Portugal in millions: 60/10 = 6/1 = 6:1.

6   Total employment/total unemployment in millions in Spain: 3/2 = 19/x; x = 12.66; 60.8% × 12.66 = 7.697 million women and 4.9627 million men unemployed.

Total employment/total unemployment in millions in Greece: $5/2 = 6/x$; $x = 2.4$; $57.5\% \times 2.4 = 1.38$ million women and 1.02 million men unemployed.

Total employment/total unemployment in millions in Germany: $9/3 = 34/x$; $x = 11.33$; $58.5\% \times 11.33 = 6.629$ million women and 4.703 million men unemployed.

Total employment/total unemployment in millions in Portugal: $2/1 = 5/x$; $x = 2.5$; $49.5\% \times 2.5 = 1.237$ million women and 1.2625 million men unemployed.

It is clear that Spain has the highest and Greece the lowest number of unemployed men.

Table 5.5 The results of six driving test centres in England

1   The total number of applicants in hundreds who passed the theoretical driving test is equal to all the applicants who took the practical driving test, whether passed or failed:

in 2001: $86 + 89 + 54 + 58 + 86 + 84 + 99 + 102 + 80 + 81 + 31 + 81 = 931$

in 2002: $119 + 191 + 66 + 68 + 109 + 112 + 101 + 111 + 45 + 50 + 10 + 20 = 1,002$

therefore the total number who passed the theoretical driving tests in 2001 and 2002 is $931 + 1,002 = 1,933$. B is the correct answer.

2   By scanning Table 5.5, you will find that only in 2001 in Warwick was the number of applicants who passed the driving test (86) higher than the number who failed the test (84). Therefore C is the correct answer.

3   The total number of applicants in hundreds who obtained a driving licence is: $119 + 66 + 109 + 101 + 45 + 10 = 450$. The percentage is $450/45 \times 100 = 10\%$. Therefore A is the correct answer.

4   By scanning the table carefully for the mentioned three choices you will find that only in Manchester did the number who failed the practical test drop year on year from 116 (1998) to 99 (1999), 96 (2000) and 58 (2001). Therefore C is the correct answer.

5   The number of applicants who obtained their driving licence in Manchester in 1998 is 100 and the number who failed the practical driving test in Hull in 2002 is 20. Therefore the ratio is 100/20 = 5:1 and B is the correct answer.

6   This can be answered by adding all who passed the driving test between 1998 and 2002 for the two chosen centres. The results in hundreds are:

Warwick: 54 + 69 + 96 + 86 + 109 = 414

London: 112 + 69 + 62 + 86 + 119 = 386

Warwick has the greatest number. Therefore A is the correct answer.

Table 5.6 Percentage increase in average family monthly expenditure since 2002 in the UK

1   The average rent increase = 11.3/100 × £600 = £67.80.

The monthly rent bill cost in 2008 = £67.80 + £600 = 667.80 ≈ £668.

2   Average increase in total expenditure in 2008 = £960 × 45/100 + £960 = £1392.

Increase in rent in 2008 = 11.3/100 × £600 + £600 = £667.80 ≈ £668.

Increase in Council Tax in 2008 = 4.5/100 × £70 + £70 = £3.15 + £70 = £73.15 ≈ £73.

Increase in bills in 2008 = 20.8/100 × £25 + £25 = £30.20 ≈ £30.

Add all the above increases in 2008 = £668 + £73 + £30 = £771.

The UK family will be left with £1392 − £771 = £621.

3   More clothing = 30 × 17/100 = +£5.1.

Less food = −130 × 7/100 = −£9.1.

Janet's monthly expenditure will differ by = −£9.1 + £5.1 = −£4.

4   The average UK family will spend the following amounts in 2008:

Rent: 600 × 11.3/100 + 600 = £667.8

Bills: 25 × 20.8/100 + 25 = £30.2

Petrol: 30 × 22.3/100 + 30 = £36.69
Council Tax: 70 × 4.5/100 + 70 = £73.15
Transport: 20 × 18.6/100 + 20 = £23.72
Clothes: 30 × 8.5/100 + 30 = £32.55
Total monthly UK family expenditure: £667.8 + £30.2 + £36.69 + £73.15 + £23.72 + £32.55 = £864.11.

5   If you add all the expenditure it will be £1,065.5. The percentage of increase = £1,065.56 − £960/£960 = 10.99% ≈ 11%.

Afterword

I hope you have enjoyed reading my book and that it has helped you to build your confidence before attending your test. Remember, if you don't do well on a test it is not the end of the world. This has nothing to do with your intelligence. Look around and you will see that many successful people probably never sat psychometric tests and might well fail if they tried to take one. It may be that you were tired or moody, or the weather affected your concentration, or possibly other environmental influences or even your genetic make-up had an effect; if so, other jobs may be more suitable for your talent. Good luck!